Longing for God

LONGING for GOD

AN INTRODUCTION TO
Christian Mysticism

WILLIAM O. PAULSELL

Paulist Press
New York / Mahwah, NJ

The Scripture quotations contained herein are from the New Revised Standard Version: Catholic Edition, Copyright © 1989 and 1993, by the Division of Christian Education of the National Council of the Churches of Christ in the United States of America. Used by permission. All rights reserved.

Cover image by Jacob_09/Shutterstock.com
Cover and book design by Lynn Else

Copyright © 2021 by William Paulsell

All rights reserved. No part of this publication may be reproduced, stored in a retrieval system, or transmitted in any form or by any means, electronic, mechanical, photocopying, recording, scanning, or otherwise, without either the prior written permission of the Publisher, or authorization through payment of the appropriate per-copy fee to the Copyright Clearance Center, Inc., www.copyright.com. Requests to the Publisher for permission should be addressed to the Permissions Department, Paulist Press, permissions@paulistpress.com.

Library of Congress Cataloging-in-Publication Data
Names: Paulsell, William O., author.
Title: Longing for God : an introduction to Christian mysticism / William O. Paulsell.
Description: New York/Mahwah : Paulist Press, 2021. | Summary: "A survey of the life and thought of Christian mystics from the time of Augustine of Hippo in the first centuries of the Church, through mediaeval times, and up to the middle of the twentieth century with Dorothy Day and Thomas Merton"— Provided by publisher.
Identifiers: LCCN 2020006691 (print) | LCCN 2020006692 (ebook) | ISBN 9780809155248 (paperback) | ISBN 9781587689192 (ebook)
Subjects: LCSH: Mystics—Biography. | Mysticism—History.
Classification: LCC BV5095.A1 P38 2021 (print) | LCC BV5095.A1 (ebook) | DDC 248.2/2—dc23
LC record available at https://lccn.loc.gov/2020006691
LC ebook record available at https://lccn.loc.gov/2020006692

ISBN 978-0-8091-5524-8 (paperback)
ISBN 978-1-58768-919-2 (e-book)

Published by Paulist Press
997 Macarthur Boulevard
Mahwah, New Jersey 07430
www.paulistpress.com

Printed and bound in the
United States of America

This book is dedicated to the memory of Professor D. Bard Thompson, who introduced me to the study of spirituality as an academic discipline.

CONTENTS

Preface ix

Acknowledgments xiii

1. What Is Mysticism? Philosophical and
   Theological Roots 1
   Philosophical Roots: Plotinus (ca. 205–270 CE) 2
   Theological Roots: Origen (ca. 185–254 CE) 4
   The Mystical Experience 9

2. Augustine (354–430): The Restless Heart Finds Peace 19

3. Bernard of Clairvaux (1090–1153): A Powerful Leader
   and Quiet Mystic 32

4. Hildegard of Bingen (1098–1179): Visionary, Healer,
   Artist, and Reformer 46

5. Meister Eckhart (ca. 1260–1327): Searching the
   Depths 58

6. Henry Suso (ca. 1295–1366): From Self-Denial
   to Simplicity 69

CONTENTS

7. John of Ruusbroec (1291–1381): Craving for God 80
8. The Quaker Tradition: The Light of God Within 89
   Rufus Jones (1863–1948) 91
   Thomas Kelly (1893–1941) 95
   Douglas Steere (1901–1995) 103
9. Howard Thurman (1899–1981): Creative Ministry 112
10. Simone Weil (1906–1943): Activist Mystic 126
11. Dorothy Day (1897–1980): A Harsh and
    Dreadful Love 141
12. Dag Hammarskjöld (1905–1961): A Hidden
    Mysticism 154
13. Thomas Merton (1915–1968): Always Searching 167
14. Mysticism and Ordinary Life 186

Notes 191

PREFACE

One by one, the monks in their white cowls walked silently into the church and found their places in the choir stalls. A bell rang and the monks began to sing the psalms in Latin with a deeply moving Gregorian chant. There were about 250 monks in those days, the late 1950s. This Protestant seminary student had never experienced anything like that, and I was deeply touched.

Bard Thompson, professor of church history at the Vanderbilt University Divinity School, took the first-year class each year to spend a day at the Abbey of Gethsemani in Kentucky, a Trappist-Cistercian monastery. We were studying medieval monasticism in our class, and Dr. Thompson wanted us to see that the institution was still alive and functioning. The schedule included attending the Divine Offices, as they called their services, meals in the guest house, a tour of the monastery, and an afternoon session with a monk who talked to us about the monastic life. We were impressed by the silence of the place and by the warm spirit of the monks.

There was always a need for people to drive on those trips and I had a car, so I went five times. On two of those visits, Thomas Merton, whose life and thought comprise the final chapter of this book, spent afternoons with us. He was gracious and in good humor, answering our questions patiently and respectfully. At the time, I did not know that he was one of the premier spiritual

LONGING FOR GOD

writers of the mid-twentieth century. Over the years I have devoured and taught most of his books.

In the 1950s, my generation of ministry students saw social action as the most important element in our vocations. We were quite caught up in the civil rights movement. African American students from Fisk and Tennessee A & I universities were engaged in an intense program of sit-ins in downtown Nashville. One of our classmates was training the students in Gandhian nonviolence and was subsequently dismissed from the university for testing segregation laws in the city. We felt tension between our desire to complete our degrees and dropping out of the university as a protest. For a variety of reasons, most of us remained.

Those Gethsemani trips opened up another dimension of the Christian life to us, one that many of us, including myself, had neglected. The sight of monks who had given up family and careers for a life of poverty, chastity, obedience, and prayer was a shock to our systems. What did they know that we did not know?

Because of the normal cycle of course offerings in the Divinity School, I had missed Dr. Thompson's course on the history of Christian spirituality. However, he agreed to do an independent study with me, and assigned readings by many of the people in this book, as well as others. That began what became a lifelong interest in spirituality in general and mysticism in particular. My specific interest gradually became the Cistercian tradition, especially the writings of Bernard of Clairvaux, who has a chapter in this book. I attended annual conferences on Cistercian history and occasionally presented papers. Some of the attendees were monks, and I learned much from them.

I never lost my social justice concerns. In fact, I published another book by Paulist Press, *Tough Minds, Tender Hearts*, which is about the spirituality of social activists. However, over the years I have developed a much deeper longing for God, as the title of this book indicates. The mystics I have studied have provided a lifetime of guidance, inspiration, and education.

Preface

On one of our trips to Gethsemani, a student asked a monk for advice on developing a deeper prayer life. The monk replied, "Do what we do, pray the Psalms." That has become a steady spiritual practice in my life, and I have learned to probe more deeply into those wonderful songs and poems.

The search for a deeper awareness of God is not easy. There are the struggles with the allure of what the world offers. There are setbacks of health, economics, relationships, and even faith, that obscure the search. But one learns to keep things in perspective and to persevere. There are moments of insight, times of serious spiritual growth, and, occasionally, a fleeting awareness of a Presence. The writers in this book will tell you that the key is love, love for God and each other. Most of them will also say that there is something deep within us untouched by the world or sin, where we can connect with the mystery of God and God's mercy, grace, forgiveness, and love.

The Abbey of Gethsemani has changed over the years. The facilities have been remodeled and improved. The community is much smaller. Several monks who became good friends and mentors have died, but it is still a remarkable place. My wife and I spend a week there on retreat each year and attend a monthly Thomas Merton discussion group often held in Merton's hermitage. Throughout the Guest House, there are many signs that say, "Silence is spoken here," a silence we find refreshing. We also find that we are not the only Protestants retreating in this beautiful Catholic setting.

I owe my own spiritual growth, which still has a long way to go, to the mystics. It is my prayer that this book will be a useful resource in fulfilling your own longing for God.

ACKNOWLEDGMENTS

There are many people to thank for making this book possible.

First, for the hospitality of the library at Lexington Theological Seminary extended by Dr. Delores Yilibow, director, and Charlie Heaberlin, archivist, where I spent many mornings researching and writing in quiet solitude. President Dr. Charisse J. Gillett welcomed a former president graciously on campus and even called to check on me when I did not show up anymore because the book was completed.

It has been a joy to work with the delightful Diane Vescovi, a senior editor at Paulist Press.

At the Abbey of Gethsemani, an institution that changed my life, I must thank Father Michael Casagram and Brother Paul Quenon, who invited me to present several conferences on mystics to the monks. Six chapters of this book had their beginnings in those conferences.

My two amazing daughters have been an important influence. Stephanie teaches courses on spirituality at Harvard Divinity School. Diane is an associate member of Holy Cross Monastery, a Benedictine Episcopal house at West Park, New York, and is studying icon painting.

LONGING FOR GOD

Most important of all is my wife, Sally, who has supported me without question in everything I have tried to do professionally and spiritually. Her doctoral research was on the conversions of major British literary figures. Having a family devoted to the study and practice of serious spirituality is a priceless treasure.

1

WHAT IS MYSTICISM?

Philosophical and Theological Roots

The very word *mysticism* conjures up images of fortune tellers, predictors of the future, and seances with the dead. This book is about none of these. It is about intelligent and thoughtful people in the mainstream of Christianity who have had continuing influence throughout history. Their writings have deepened the faith of many and provided guidance for spiritual growth. Most were orthodox in their theology. Thomas Merton, who is regarded as a twentieth-century mystic, wrote, "There is no question that the mystics are the ones who have kept Christianity going, if anyone has."[1]

Merton wrote this in a letter in 1963, when thoughtful people were becoming disenchanted with Christianity, particularly as it was found in many local churches. The churches seemed superficial, too much an expression of American culture and its social, political, and economic values. Some people wanted a deeper religious experience. They sought guidance on the inner life. They dared to explore the depths of their souls. They were not after stronger belief; they were searching for the essence of religion found in many traditions and practices.

Not finding these things in their churches, they turned to the East. They developed an interest in Buddhism, particularly the Zen expression of it. They looked at Sufism, the mystical form of Islam. They searched for Hindu holy men. They began to talk about enlightenment, about karma, about how the Tao moves through human life. They wanted to find a guru, a rinpoche, a lama, a monk, a rabbi, an imam, who could teach them the deeper mysteries.

Some began to explore mysticism, an oft-neglected component of all major religions. There are Jewish, Hindu, Buddhist, and Islamic as well as Christian mystics. Mysticism is as old as religion itself. W. R. Inge in his classic book *Christian Mysticism* called mysticism "the raw material of all religion."[2] Religions begin because someone has an encounter with the Divine.

What these seekers did not realize was that what they were looking for could be found in the Christian mystical tradition. Christian spirituality is broad and deep. The writer of the Letter to the Ephesians encouraged the readers to explore "the breadth and length and height and depth" of Christian experience and to know the love of Christ that "surpasses knowledge" (Eph 3:18–19). This is what mystics seek, that which surpasses all rational knowledge and leads to truth.

PHILOSOPHICAL ROOTS: PLOTINUS (CA. 205–270 CE)

An Egyptian sat by a window reading a book written by the Greek philosopher Plato in the middle of the fourth century BCE. He might have been trying to understand why this ancient philosopher denied the reality of individual things. After all, he saw objects all around him: the room in which he was reading, the furniture where he sat and ate and rested, the clay jars in the kitchen, the trees and plants outside his window. He knew they

What Is Mysticism?

were real. He could see and touch them. When he left home, they would still be there when he returned.

We know little about Plotinus's early life. He apparently grew up in Alexandria, received a classical education, and, it is believed, made a journey to the East to learn Oriental philosophy. As Plotinus studied Plato's writings, he began to understand that physical things are not real, only the ideas of them are real. Physical things change and deteriorate, but ideas are forever. Eventually, he moved to Rome and set up a school where he taught what came to be known as Neoplatonism, a religious philosophy that was a major influence in the development of Christian mysticism.

Plotinus was not a Christian, but Christians were heavily influenced by him. There existed for him a "great chain of being," beginning with what he called the One or the Idea of the Good, or God, whose nature overflowed, or emanated, into lesser realms of reality. These included the *Nous*, Plato's realm of ideas, the World Soul, which is intelligence, and then finally, matter, the most unreal level of all. One of the problems with matter is that it draws us away from the One.

Humans may have a longing for the eternal and unchanging, the One, but they are caught in matter, physical bodies. The way back to the One is intellectual and spiritual contemplation that liberates one from dependence upon the world of sense and leads to the intelligible world. The whole system is understood in terms of falling and rising, working one's way back up the "great chain of being." Some describe it as "the journey of the mind to God," or a mystical union with the One.

Plotinus wrote nothing until about age fifty when he set down the lectures he had given in his school, a series of treatises called *Enneads*. Bernard McGinn describes them as "among the greatest masterpieces of mystical as well as of philosophical literature."[3] Plotinus was a mystic. His student Porphyry said that he was with Plotinus when he had four mystical experiences over a period of six years.

THEOLOGICAL ROOTS: ORIGEN (CA. 185–254 CE)

The third century was a time of considerable persecution of Christians in the Roman Empire. Emperors were determined to maintain cultural unity, and, when Christians refused to offer sacrifices to Roman gods, they were regarded as treasonous. Many were imprisoned, others exiled, and some were martyred. One such martyr was the father of a man who would later become an important theologian, biblical scholar, and mystical writer—Origen. The oft-told story is that when he was a boy he wanted to be martyred as his father had been in 202, but his mother prevented it by hiding his clothes. Later in life, he was imprisoned and brutally tortured during a persecution and later died because of his injuries.

Origen taught Christian faith in a catechetical school in Alexandria, Egypt. When he became the head of the school, he adopted a life of strict self-denial, including fasting, long vigils, and voluntary poverty. He traveled to Rome and Arabia, and later to Palestine, where he was asked to preach. Since he was a layman without authority to do so, he was recalled to Alexandria by his bishop. He then focused his attention on writing, and was later ordained in Palestine. His bishop in Alexandria deposed him from the priesthood because of what he thought were irregularities in his ordination, whereupon Origen moved to Caesarea and established a school, where he continued writing and preaching. He wrote commentaries on the Bible and put together the Hexapla, which consisted of six Greek versions of parts of the Old Testament in parallel columns. His best-known writings were *On First Principles*, *On Prayer*, and *Exhortation to Martyrdom*. Many

What Is Mysticism?

of his writings did not survive, partly because of accusations of heresy. Of particular interest in this chapter is his commentary on the Song of Songs.

Origen was foremost a scripture scholar. His commentaries went verse by verse in explaining the moral and spiritual meaning of the Bible. He was by no means a literalist and was way ahead of his time in that regard. That gave him the freedom to explore meanings below the surface of the text. Even if a passage referenced something that did not actually happen, there was a deeper spiritual meaning to be found there.

In his book *On First Principles*, Origen wrote about his non-literal approach to the Bible. "To what person of intelligence," he wrote, "would the Genesis 1 creation story make any sense when on each of the first three days we are told there was evening and there was morning when the sun and moon had not yet been created." When in Genesis 3 we are told that God "is said to stroll in the garden in the afternoon," Origen said that is "the form of a type by which they point to certain mysteries." How could the devil actually show Jesus all the kingdoms of the world from one mountaintop? Origen did not take the passages literally, but behind all such passages Origen saw a deep spiritual meaning.[4]

When he wrote about the ascent to God, there is the implication of a prior descent, which we have seen in Neoplatonism. The history of Israel in the Old Testament, as Origen read it, is actually about the fall and rise of souls. Origen said that just as humans have bodies, souls, and spirits, so the Bible has the same. The common and historical understanding of Scripture is the body. People who advance spiritually and see the Bible in broader terms, have found the soul of the Bible. Those who have progressed spiritually and found what Paul called the "secret and hidden wisdom of God" have found the spirit of Scripture.[5]

A standard outline used by mystical writers to describe the assent to God has three stages. The first is the purgative way, where we attempt to purge from our lives those things that obscure our ascent to God. Second was the illuminative way, where we grow in our knowledge of God and spiritual truth. Third is the unitive way, mystical union with God, the meaning of which will be discussed later. Origen saw the three books of Solomon as illustrative of these three steps. Proverbs teaches us how to live moral and virtuous lives, the purgative way. Ecclesiastes teaches us about the nature of things and how to make proper use of them, the illuminative way. The Song of Songs generates a desire (*eros*) and a love for God, the unitive way.

The lovers in the Song find deep joy when they are together and are unhappy when apart. There is obvious erotic imagery in the Song of Songs: the wound of love, this kiss of lovers, the embrace, the couch, the bed. Bernard McGinn says that Origen made a daring breakthrough when he suggested that God must be *Eros* "if the *eros*, desire, implanted in us is what returns us to him."[6] In relation to this desire, Origen described the two creations of humans. In Genesis 1, we are made in the image of God. He called that the inner person. In Genesis 2, we are made from the "dust of the ground," the outer person. He then referred to Paul's comment: "Even though our outer nature is wasting away, our inner nature is being renewed day by day" (2 Cor 4:16). Paul also expressed it another way: "I delight in the law of God in my inmost self, but I see in my members another law at war with the law of my mind" (Rom 7:22–23). Our inner nature desires to rise to God; our outer nature—the physical body—holds us back.

Origen drew an allegorical parallel to this in his commentary on the Song of Songs, which he called "a drama of mystical meaning."[7] A few examples will illustrate Origen's use of allegory. The first verse of the Song immediately gets our attention: "Let him kiss me with the kisses of his mouth." The woman longs for her lover and pleads, "Draw me after you, let us make haste." She wants his kisses and she wants them now: "Make haste!"

That is the surface meaning. Origen saw much more in that verse than just a woman wanting passionate kisses from her lover.

What Is Mysticism?

This is an allegory of the Church longing for union with Christ. The Church had received many premarital gifts: the law and the prophets revealed the Son of God to whom the Church was betrothed. These gifts taught her many things about Christ: his being filled with the Holy Spirit, his acts and power and works, his charm and gentleness, that she might burn with love for him. She has seen his ministers, but she has not seen him. Angels and prophets are not enough. She wants him and the kisses of his mouth. She wants his words poured into her mouth, "that I may hear him speak himself and see him teaching."[8]

Then Origen shifted the focus from the Church to the individual. "Let us bring in the soul whose only desire is to be united to the Word of God made flesh and to be in fellowship with him, and to enter into the mysteries of his wisdom and knowledge." She had knowledge from her masters and teachers, but this did not satisfy her desire and love. Now she wants Christ himself. When she has begun to understand what was obscure and "unravel what was tangled," then she knew that she had received the kisses of Christ himself, the Word of God. When we search for the meaning of something and cannot find it, we can pray, "Let him kiss me with the kisses of his mouth."

Another verse we do not normally expect to find in the Bible is, "Your breasts are better than wine, and the fragrance of thine ointments is above all spices." This is Origen's translation. The New Revised Standard Version (NRSV) softens this by translating it: "Your love is better than wine, and your anointing oils are fragrant" (Song 1:2–3). Origen's version is more interesting.

The breasts in question are those of the bridegroom, who arrived while she was praying for kisses. Shirtless, or in some other way, he has revealed his breasts to her, anointed with ointment and having a fragrance that is pleasing to the bride. Now, instead of praying for kisses she is moved by the beauty of his breasts and says, "Thy breasts are better than wine, and the fragrance of thine ointments is above all spices."[9] That is the literal meaning, but what is the inner meaning? The issue is the ground of the heart. In John 13, Origen reminds us, the disciple whom Jesus loved reclined on the breast of Jesus. That scene has been portrayed in Christian art over the centuries. The King James Version says, "Now there was leaning on Jesus's bosom one of the disciples, whom Jesus loved." The NRSV is more cautious and translates, "One of his disciples—the one whom Jesus loved—was reclining next to him" (v. 23).

The ground of the heart is symbolized by the breast of the bridegroom. That heart, wrote Origen, "surpasses all the wine that is wont to gladden man's heart." The bridegroom's heart has treasures of wisdom and knowledge concealed in it. In Scripture, several types of wine are mentioned. Origen regards these as referencing several kinds of teaching, but the heart of the bridegroom, who is Christ, is superior to even the best wine.

"The fragrance of thine ointments is above all spices" (Song 1:3). Or, "Your anointing oils are fragrant, your name is perfume poured out" (NRSV). The fragrance of the bridegroom delights the bride. As a young woman she had used a variety of spices on herself, by which she means, according to Origen, the law and the prophets. But when the bridegroom appeared, she realized that her own fragrances were inferior and she could only say, "The fragrance of thine ointments is above all spices." Origen quoted from Ephesians that the washing water of the gospel will present the church to Christ "without a spot or wrinkle or anything of the kind" (Eph 5:26–27).

Many mystics have treated the Song of Songs in the same way. Below the surface meaning are deep spiritual truths. The reason for this is easy to understand when we consider that the mystical experience has everything to do with union with God in Christ, in an encounter that surpasses rationality and words to describe it.

In both Plotinus and Origen, we see the development of a spiritual pattern that will be standard in the mystical life: rising and falling. There are times in our lives when we reach the heights of religious experience. At other times we experience the absence of God. We are in the desert. We have a longing for God, but God is nowhere to be found. The experience is painful, and it can threaten our faith. Fourteen mystics in the following chapters will act as guides, offering insights and teaching us how the mystical experience strengthened their faith. But first, what is the "mystical experience"? And is it relevant to our lives in this day and age?

THE MYSTICAL EXPERIENCE

There have been many claims of mystical experience that have included visions, hearing voices, being transported to another realm, and some bizarre emotions. Quaker mystic Rufus Jones, however, was skeptical of these. He said that he was cautious about expecting "secret messages from sociable angels."[10] Hildegard of Bingen had visions, but Bernard of Clairvaux said that his senses experienced nothing when he had an encounter with God. Thomas Merton wrote a graphic description of his experience in Cuba. He was convinced that God was right there in front of him, but there was no sensory experience. What many mystics wanted was not a vision, but God.

What, then, is a mystic? There are many definitions, some of which will be explored in the following chapters. The simplest and most basic definition is that a mystic is a person who has experienced the presence of God in a very direct way. The event is so real and certain that there can be no doubt about what happened. However, mystics throughout the centuries have found it impossible to communicate the experience to the rest of us. Human language fails in its effort. God is beyond all language, all definition, all modes of expression. The people who will be presented in this book tried to tell us what the experience was like, but, in one way or another, they found it impossible to put it into words.

LONGING FOR GOD

Mysticism assumes that the human mind is capable of reaching beyond the physical world, beyond the limitations of our five senses and our rational thinking. F. C. Happold saw it as "a break through the world of time and history into one of eternity and timelessness."[11] It is a transcendent experience that crosses the usual boundaries of thought, language, and knowledge. Many mystics will tell you that in the experience they did not see, hear, taste, touch, or smell anything. It was beyond sensory experience and beyond the limitations of reason. Some had visions but many of the people we will study did not see such things as necessary.

Bernard McGinn, in his excellent seven-volume history of Western Christian mysticism, understands mysticism three ways: (1) mysticism as an element of religion; (2) mysticism as a process or way of life; and (3) mysticism as an attempt to express a direct consciousness of the presence of God.[12] For him, the unifying note in Christian mysticism is the term *presence*.

William James, in his classic *Varieties of Religious Experience*, outlined four basic characteristics or "marks" of mystical experience:[13]

1. **Ineffable**: "No reports of its contents can be given in words." Language fails here. It cannot be described to another person. Mystics knew that no description of God could be adequate to explain who or what God is. Such a vocabulary does not exist. That is not a problem for mystics. They would rather be caught up in the overpowering and transforming mystery of God.
2. **Noetic**: It generates knowledge, but it is not an experience that can be generated by using reason. It goes beyond the limits of reason and takes the mystic into new ways of knowing. This is a knowledge that cannot be learned, only experienced.

What Is Mysticism?

3. **Transient**: It is temporary, and often brief, although the mystic loses all sense of time until it is over. The subsequent absence of God is frustrating, and the mystic wants God to come back. Still, the mystic is grateful that for one brief moment the presence of God was so real that it could not be doubted.
4. **Passive**: No one can make it happen. It comes upon a person unexpectedly. The mystic senses that his or her own will is not functioning at all. One may have a sense of being taken over by God. The general consensus of mystics is that it is an unearned and unmerited gift of God.

Christians will ask, Is there mysticism in the Bible? The answer is clearly *yes*. Today biblical scholarship is built on what is called historical criticism. The word *criticism* is used in the sense of literary criticism, where a critic will analyze a novel or a poem. Biblical critics will ask a series of questions: when was a particular passage written, who wrote it, what was the intended audience, where was it written, what literary style was used, what is the nature of the text, what does the use of language tell us, how does it reflect the culture in which it was written?

Medieval biblical scholars took a different approach. They saw layers of meaning behind what we see on the surface. They searched for the literal meaning, the moral meaning, the allegorical meaning, and the spiritual or mystical meaning. Biblical writers found it impossible to express the deepest truths in normal language, so they used mythical language to express the inexpressible. For centuries writers have used myth to express ideas that were impossible to express in any other way. Many mystics said that only a spiritual reading of the Bible can reveal its full intent.

One of the writers of Genesis tells us that Moses encountered God in a burning bush and in the darkness on the Mount Sinai summit. For mystics, God is often encountered in darkness.

LONGING FOR GOD

Fire is a frequently used image to express religious experience in the Bible. John the Baptist told his hearers that he will baptize them with water, but Jesus will baptize them with "the Holy Spirit and fire" (Matt 3:11). In the story of Pentecost, we are told that a tongue of fire rested on each of the apostles (Acts 2:3). The writer of the Letter to the Hebrews affirmed that "indeed our God is a consuming fire" (12:29). Mythical images are often essential for expressing the inexpressible. Fire is very powerful. We often regard it as destructive. Mystics saw it as an image of purification.

Isaiah tells us that he saw God high and lifted up in the temple (Isa 6:1). All kinds of mythical images are used to express his mystical experience: a throne, a vestment that filled the temple, seraphim, smoke, a live coal in a pair of tongs that touches the prophet's lips and purifies him. These images impress us with the depth and power of Isaiah's undefinable encounter with God. The experience is interpreted as a call to the prophetic vocation. Mystical experiences often result in a radical change in the direction of a life.

Two of his disciples experienced Jesus transfigured before them and felt overwhelmed. The writer of the Gospel of Matthew attempted to describe the experience. He used powerful images: Jesus's face "shone like the sun" and his clothing was "dazzling white." Bright light is often a part of mystical experience. Other historical figures appeared: Moses and Elijah. There was a bright cloud over the setting, as well as a heavenly voice. Peter and James had a new insight into who Jesus was. How does a writer express that? Put these images together and you have a powerful expression of an encounter with the Divine. The experience did not last long—it was transient. At the end, Peter and James looked up and "saw no one except Jesus himself alone" (Matt 17:1–8). His appearance was back to normal.

The great missionary doctor Albert Schweitzer wrote a number of controversial books. Best known for his magisterial *Quest of the Historical Jesus*, he also wrote *The Mysticism of Paul the Apostle*.

What Is Mysticism?

Schweitzer said that whenever Christianity attempts to understand the relationship of God to the world, "it cannot help opening the door to mysticism."[14] For mystics, Paul is a rich source. Paul heard Jesus on the road to Damascus, and in one of his letters he tells of rising to the third heaven and even Paradise itself. However, Schweitzer noted that Paul falls short of classical mysticism in that he never writes about being one with God. In fact, he said that Paul does not have a God-mysticism, but only a Christ-mysticism. It is through our encounter with Christ that one comes into a relationship with God. Schweitzer cited Galatians 2:20: "It is no longer I who live, but it is Christ who lives in me." At the end of his book, he wrote, "Paul's greatest achievement was to grasp, as the thing essential to be a Christian, the experience of union with Christ."[15]

There are three stories of Paul's conversion written by Luke in the Book of Acts and one by Paul himself in his letter to the Galatians. In Luke's account, three versions are found in Acts: 9:1–18; 22:6–21; and 26:12–23. The two images used in these stories are light, which surprised Paul, and a voice that, in the third version, spoke Hebrew. Paul's own account is that God is "pleased to reveal his Son to me" (Gal 1:13–17) and Paul was converted—a simple statement of fact with no mythical images.

In 2 Corinthians 12, Paul wrote of a person being "caught up to the third heaven' and even "into Paradise." He was not sure if this was an in-the-body or out-of-body experience. Third heaven and Paradise are mythical expressions, which Paul used because he could find no other way to express the experience. In fact, he said that the person heard things "that are not to be told, that no mortal is permitted to repeat." If that is the case, he had to find some other way to tell us what happened. So, he drew upon these images, knowing that they were not adequate to describe what was experienced.

What is it that motivates a mystic? It is true that mystics are surprised by an unexpected experience. No one can force it or make it happen. Ultimately, it is a gift of God. Karen Armstrong

LONGING FOR GOD

in her book *The Spiral Staircase* tells of her desire to become a mystic. She joined a religious order and became a nun. She tried very hard, but it never happened, so she gave up and left the order. Jean Leclerq's *The Love of Learning and the Desire for God* described programs of education for medieval monks that might help fulfill the longing for God that so many had. But there was no guarantee of mystical perception. There is, however, in the hearts of many, if not most mystics, a deep desire and longing for God. We find that expressed with considerable frequency in the Book of Psalms. Through the centuries, the Book of Psalms has been the prayer book of Christianity. Praying psalms is a spiritual discipline practiced by many. It is the staple of monastic prayer. For example, the beginning of Psalm 42 reflects the longing of many religious people:

> As a deer longs for flowing streams,
>   so my soul longs for you, O God.
> My soul thirsts for God,
>   for the living God.
> When shall I come and behold
>   the face of God?

Psalm 130:6 describes the waiting that all religious people do:

> My soul waits for the Lord
>   more than those who watch for the morning.

We pray and there seems to be no response, so we wait as impatiently as the sleepy night watchman waits for the sun to rise so he can go home. We wait by the bed of a sick loved one, we wait for the job we want, we wait for a relationship to develop into permanence, we wait for someone to grow and mature, we wait for the forgiveness of a friend we have offended, we wait for justice and peace, we wait for God's self-revelation in our life. We

What Is Mysticism?

hope that in this waiting we will catch a glimpse of what God is doing.

An important passage in Scripture for mystics is the story of Mary and Martha (Luke 10:38–42). The two sisters welcomed Jesus into their home. Mary sat on the floor at the feet of Jesus in that humble little house and listened very attentively to everything Jesus said. Martha was busy in the kitchen, perhaps preparing a meal for the three of them, and needed assistance. She told Jesus to tell Mary to come help her get ready. But Jesus said, "Mary has chosen the better part." Martha thought she was doing well by taking care of the practicalities of the visit. Jesus, however, rebuked her, telling her that she was letting herself be distracted from what he had to say. "There is need of only one thing," he told her. Martha was too distracted to listen to the gospel from the Source.

Distractions in the spiritual life are always frustrating. Mystics engage in a variety of spiritual disciplines in an attempt to minimize them. That is what drove the early desert fathers and mothers away from the cities and towns of the Roman Empire. It is what led people into monasteries and convents. It is what caused some to simplify their lives. All of the mystics we will study here wrestled with the same issues. Distractions were always with them and, in some cases, were intensified when they tried to defeat them. The desert fathers and mothers fled the cities of Rome in the hope of reducing temptation, only to find that in the desert the temptations were more intense.

As mentioned already, the Song of Songs, sometimes known as the Song of Solomon, is enormously significant for mystics. In fact, in the Middle Ages, it was regarded as the textbook for mysticism and was commented on more frequently than any other book of the Bible. Many mystics wrote commentaries on the Song, finding levels of meaning that might escape the average reader. It was seen as the key to unlocking the essential meaning of the Bible, God's love for us. As one commentator stated, "It was a fathomless pool of

LONGING FOR GOD

meaning one could swim in one's whole life long and never sound the bottom. It was a garden in which one might encounter God walking in the cool of the day."[16] A reader new to the Song might see it as an erotic love poem where two lovers praise each other, pursue each other, long for each other, and find joy in each other. For mystics, much more was there than what one might see on the surface. The Song had depths yet to be plumbed.

The two lovers find joy in each other when they are together and intensely long for each other when apart. Some mystics saw in this the alternations of the spiritual life. There are times when God seems clearly present to us; at other times, we know God only by God's absence, which is painful. God seems to come and go. There is the ecstasy of contemplation, as well as the dark night of the soul. There will be references to the Song of Songs in some of what the mystics being studied here wrote. Although God is never actually mentioned in the Song, many wrote commentaries and homilies, finding God throughout it.

How do we know whether a religious experience we have is from God or is just an illusion? That is a fundamental question in our subject. There are many answers people have given over time. Some would say it is authentic if it is in continuity with Scripture. Others would say it is valid if it is an expression of the gospel. Many would answer the question by asking, How does it affect your life? Does it make you a better person? Are you a more loving, compassionate, merciful, forgiving person? If you are, it was probably something that came from God. If, however, an experience led you to believe that you alone had the truth and you became hostile, critical, judgmental, and angry toward others, it was likely an illusion and not authentic.

This is not to say that all mystics are perfect examples of what a religious person should be. Everyone is human, and the human condition seems to work against perfection. Many mystics are considered to be saints, but that does not mean they are not flawed. All of us are flawed to one degree or another. An intimate

What Is Mysticism?

encounter with God can be the pinnacle of the religious life, but it does not destroy human weakness. Paul said, "I can will what is right, but I cannot do it. For I do not do the good I want, but the evil I do not want is what I do" (Rom 7:18–19).

So, mysticism is a mixed bag. Some mystics had serious health issues. Bernard of Clairvaux had constant stomach problems. Hildegard of Bingen had illnesses that seemed to create an opening to visions. Simone Weil had terrible headaches. Thomas Merton was plagued with back and skin problems.

Why should we study mystics at all? Jesus told us to feed the hungry, give the thirsty a drink, welcome the stranger, clothe the naked, care for the sick, and visit the prisoner. The fact is that a person with no religious faith at all can do all of those things. When they are done out of a deep relationship with God, those good works have a different character, a different spirit about them, a different motivation behind them, a different depth to them. They bring the reality of God into the lives of the people we serve even if they do not recognize it. Some of the mystics we will look at in this book were dedicated social activists. The ideal, of course, is for our lives to have a balance of contemplation and activism.

Mystics believed that the way to achieve that ideal is found in a single verse in the Sermon on the Mount: "Blessed are the pure in heart, for they will see God" (Matt 5:8). Purity of heart is a challenge for every religious person, and mystical writers come back to that verse again and again. Attaining purity of heart in the midst of our distractions is a continuing struggle. Trying to develop a heart of love, compassion, and mercy is a lifetime challenge. Knowing a God whom the gospel tells us is a God of love calls for a purity we may never fully attain, but that purity stands before us as a constant goal.

Let us begin our journey studying some of the greatest and best-known mystics. They have much to teach us about developing our own spiritual lives. We will find some ideas helpful; others will be beyond us. The most important thing is discovering that it is possible to actually know the presence of God in our lives, that there can be contact between the human and the Divine. It is one thing to have a faith based on a body of doctrine, but it is quite another to build our faith on the experience of God's presence in our lives. It is a matter of seeing reality as it actually is, not as others want us to see it. William James said, "The range of mystical experience is very wide."[17]

FURTHER READING

Origen. *An Exhortation to Martyrdom, Prayer, and Selected Works.* Translated by Rowan A. Greer. The Classics of Western Spirituality. New York: Paulist Press, 1979.

Origen. *The Song of Songs, Commentary, and Homilies.* Edited by Johannes Quasten, STD, and Joseph C. Plumpe. Translated by R. P. Lawson. Ancient Christian Writers, vol. 26. Westminster, MD: Newman Press, 1957.

2
AUGUSTINE
354–430
The Restless Heart Finds Peace

Mother and son stood looking out a window at the garden of a country house at Ostia. They needed a place, away from the city of Milan, where they could think things through. A friend had loaned them this house. Something momentous had recently happened, and in their conversation, they were trying to understand what it meant. The son had built a reputation as an outstanding teacher of rhetoric. Would he continue in that profession, or would his new life bring about change? Would this change last, or would it, like many other resolutions in his life, fade away as he moved on to something else? Mother was a devout Christian and wanted her son to embrace the Church, but like many children, he had resisted her insistent admonitions. He had read philosophy and joined the Manichaeans, who saw human problems as a constant battle between evil flesh and good spirit. In time he found the sect unsatisfying and came under the influence of a Catholic bishop whom he found impressive, although he wondered how any man could live a celibate life.

LONGING FOR GOD

The bishop's preaching opened a new direction in life for the son, which ultimately led to a powerful emotional and tearful conversion experience. The son then resigned as a professor of rhetoric in Milan, where he had taught lawyers to argue their cases and orators how to be more spellbinding.

As mother and son tried to make sense of this sudden development, something strange began to happen. The son had spent most of his life trying to satisfy his sexual urges, but now he saw that finding God was a much greater pleasure. Suddenly, together they had an experience of rising in their minds above "all corporeal things," ascending "through heaven itself from which the sun, moon, and stars shine upon the earth." They passed beyond their own minds, he said, and rose even higher in their thoughts as they pondered God and all God's works. Then they briefly touched Wisdom with the whole effort of their hearts, and the son's life was changed forever. The mother would soon die, satisfied that her desires for her son had been fulfilled. The experience, as is usually the case with mystical experiences, was brief, after which they descended, returning to the sound of their conversation.[1]

My first introduction to mysticism was hearing the word spoken by a college English professor as she lectured about poets, but I did not really understand what it meant until I read *Confessions*. Augustine answered my questions. Now I saw a new meaning to his most famous quotation from the beginning of his *Confessions*: "You have made us for yourself, O God, and our hearts are restless until they rest in you." Reading Augustine gave me a deeper understanding of what Christian faith is about and stimulated my interest in deeper religious experience. Augustine's *Confessions* does contain confessions of sin, but more importantly, it is a confession of faith.

Augustine discovered that the reality of God can be experienced by humans. It is possible to touch Wisdom, to open our awareness of the transcendent, to experience a Divine Presence.

Augustine

Being assigned *Confessions* in a seminary class altered my perception of religion and stimulated a lifelong interest in mysticism. I had never heard this in the church where I was very active as a youth, but Augustine changed my life. I never became a mystic, but studying the lives of mystics became a source of inspiration and maturing faith.

Dom Cuthbert Butler in his fine book *Western Mysticism* saw Augustine as "the greatest genius of Western Christianity." He also described him as "the Prince of Mystics," who had "the most penetrating intellectual vision into things divine and a love of God that was a consuming passion."[2] Passion is an apt description of his personality. Whatever he did, he did it with tireless energy, enthusiasm, and, yes, passion. He sinned with passion, he searched for truth with passion, he converted with passion, he built a theology with passion, he opposed his doctrinal critics with passion, and he served as a bishop with passion. His most passionate book, originally titled *Confessions in Thirteen Books*, is also his best known. Modern English translations sometimes give it the title *The Confessions of Saint Augustine*.

According to Bernard McGinn, who called Augustine "the founding Father of Western mysticism," Augustine produced more writings than could ever be read by most modern readers.[3] Most important for us are *Confessions*, *Homilies on the Psalms*, and books eight through fifteen of *On The Trinity*, all of which add to our knowledge of Augustine's mysticism. Scholars see these as important sources for understanding the mystical life. There are, of course, many more.

Augustine was born in 354 in the small North African town of Tagaste, known as Souk Ahras in today's Algeria, located sixty miles inland from the Mediterranean Sea, on the southern edge of the Roman Empire. It was a Roman town of a few thousand people who lived off the land as farmers. It was a part of Numida, also known as Rome's granary. It had the usual Roman infrastructure: roads, amphitheaters, and aqueducts. The town was under the administration of Carthage, far to the East. In an earlier century the area had been prosperous, but by Augustine's day it was in economic decline. There were families of wealth, but most lived hard lives of labor and deprivation. Ten years before Augustine's birth, there had been a peasants' revolt in the south. During his life, the Roman Empire was crumbling as barbarians from Scandinavia and the steppes of Russia began to invade the frontiers. At the end of Augustine's life in 430, the Visigoths would be attacking North Africa, and in a few decades, the Roman Empire in the West would be no more.[4]

The area was Roman Catholic. Early in life Augustine was a nominal Christian, who attended church occasionally, but was dissatisfied with the institution, did not take it very seriously, and was not baptized. He read parts of the Bible but concluded that it was inferior to the Greek and Roman classics.

His father, Patricius, was a minor official, a decurion, whose main duty was tax collecting. He did own a few vineyards worked by slaves, but generally his economic situation was precarious. The only hope for Augustine was a classical education. His father made financial sacrifices to provide it, but during one year, Augustine had to drop out of school for a lack of funding. A local man of wealth, Romanianus, patronized young Augustine. As Peter Brown put it in his fine biography, "luck and talent" enabled Augustine to prosper, becoming a prestigious professor in Milan and, ultimately, a Catholic bishop in North Africa.[5] A number of young men in the town went off to seek their fortunes, but some would eventually return to North Africa as bishops in small towns.

Augustine's mother, Monica, according to Brown, dominated his inner life. She was a devout Christian who had been the voice of God for him, urging him to accept the faith. Her deepest desire was that Augustine become a baptized Christian, and she lived just long enough to see that happen. Earlier, her husband had converted, shortly before his death.

Augustine

Years later, in 401, as Augustine looked back over his life while composing *Confessions*, he wrote about the restless heart resting in God. It was many years before Augustine would have the knowledge and experience to write those words.

His youth was such that no one would have expected him to become a saint. In his young life he enjoyed of a variety of sins. He stole from his parents so he could trade food for the toys of others. Writing *Confessions*, he expressed to God his regret that he had wasted his God-given mental powers and admitted that his "shameful passions" had led him far from God. He regretted that he could not "distinguish the serenity of love from the fog of lust."[6]

In an oft-told story from his boyhood, he joined his friends in the dark of night to steal some pears from a neighbor's orchard. The theft was not done out of need. He had plenty at home and, more than that, the fruit he already had was of much better quality. What made this deed even worse was throwing away what he had picked. "Our pleasure lay in doing what was not allowed," he wrote. The others threw theirs at some hogs. He concluded, "I had no motive for my wickedness except wickedness itself."[7]

A theft of a few pears seems like a fairly harmless teenage prank, but for Augustine it was an example of human nature. We are drawn to evil for the excitement of doing it. He wrote that the pleasure was "in the crime itself, done in association with a sinful group." Years later as Augustine reflected on the incident, he realized that it was not a trivial prank, it was an example of our nature. We are drawn to evil, and only the grace of God can transform us and save us from it. Discovering the origin of evil became an obsession with Augustine, and it led him through a variety of philosophical and religious ideas as he sought answers.

He moved to Carthage to further his education, where, he said, "All around me hissed a cauldron of illicit loves."[8] He described his soul as being "in rotten health." What he wanted was to love and be loved, particularly if he could enjoy the body

LONGING FOR GOD

of someone. "I therefore polluted the spring water of friendship with the filth of concupiscence," he wrote. "I muddied its clear stream by the hell of lust."[9] He had moral battles to fight. He was a success in school, at the top of his class in rhetoric. He said, "I wanted to distinguish myself as an orator for the damnable and conceited purpose, namely delight in human vanity."[10]

One of the most important events in Augustine's life took place in this context. He read a book by Cicero, *Hortensius*, which convinced him that the most important thing in life is to seek after truth. The book no longer exists, except for quotations in Augustine's writings. But it changed his life. "It gave me different values and priorities. I began to rise up and return to [God]."[11] The return began slowly and had a long way to go. God was still far distant. Augustine tried reading the Bible, but found it inferior to the writings of Cicero.

Augustine was still concerned about the source of evil. Why is it so difficult for us to resist? He was soon to find an explanation that would satisfy him at least temporarily. The sect known as Manichaeism attracted Augustine's attention for nine years. Founded by Mani, who lived in the third century, it began in Persia. It saw the world in dualistic terms: light or darkness, spirit or the material world. The two are at constant war with each other. Evil is rooted in the material part of ourselves. Our bodies are the problem, not our minds, an idea that greatly interested Augustine in explaining his own moral problems. It combined ideas from a variety of Eastern religious movements and spread widely, emphasizing self-denial as a way of combating evil. It had a complicated mythology, which Augustine later rejected.

In Carthage, Augustine became a teacher of rhetoric. At the same time, he found a mistress to whom he was faithful for seventeen years. They never married, and he said that he learned the difference between a marriage that wanted a family and a relationship between two people whose love was solely a matter of pleasure. The couple who did not want to have children, did, however, produce a son, Adeodatus, whom Augustine came to love deeply.

In time, Augustine became disillusioned with Manichaeism. He had many questions that no one in the sect could answer, not even Faustus, a highly respected Manichaean teacher, who should have been able to answer all his questions when they met together. However, the encounter was a disappointment. Faustus had a warm heart and spoke with great eloquence, but, Augustine realized, was not well educated in the liberal arts. Augustine said that having a fine style did not mean that what Faustus said was true.[12] He gave up on the Manichees in his quest to find something that was unchangeable—the Manichees could not provide it.[13]

Soon thereafter, Augustine moved to Rome to teach. His mother had strongly objected, but he boarded a ship while she was praying and left in the middle of the night accompanied by his faithful mistress and his son. His primary motivation for moving was that students in Rome were more disciplined and went quietly about their studies, whereas students in Carthage were "foul and uncontrolled." They disrupted classes and committed vandalism "with an astonishing mindlessness."[14] On later reflection, Augustine realized that God wanted him to go to Rome, but the influence of the Manichees was difficult to leave behind.

Because of their dualistic theology, Augustine thought of God as a physical mass and believed that everything that existed was material. Likewise, he saw evil as a material substance, something malignant "creeping through the earth."[15] These ideas continued to trouble him. Meanwhile, he discovered that students in Rome found ways to avoid paying their tuition. Seeking more financial security, he learned that there was an opening for a teacher of rhetoric in Milan, where he applied and was accepted. He took his faithful lover and Adeodatus with him. Milan was a major city, the residence of the Roman Emperor, Valentinian II.

This was the most important move of Augustine's life, for it put him in touch with Ambrose, the bishop of Milan, "known

LONGING FOR GOD

throughout the world as among the best of men." It was he who would lead Augustine to God. He decided to become a catechumen in the Church until, he said, some clear light would direct what he should do.

His mother joined him in Milan, finding him depressed because he seemed to have lost hope of discovering the truth. He was no longer a Manichee but was not a Catholic either. He wrote, "I had not yet attained the truth, but I was rescued from falsehood."[16] He continued to admire Ambrose but thought his celibacy must be painful. Gradually, however, Augustine became more interested in the Church. "Little by little," he wrote, "Lord, with a most gentle and merciful hand you touched and calmed my heart."[17] Because of Ambrose's skill as an interpreter, Augustine developed a new appreciation for the Bible, which he had formerly regarded as inferior literature.

Augustine began to read Neoplatonism, a philosophy built on the writings of Plotinus, who thought of God as the One from which all things begin and from which they emanate, or fall. The farther away things fall from the One, the more material they are. The goal of the religious person is to rise back toward the One, which is pure spirit. Reading this encouraged Augustine to look within what he called "my innermost citadel." With his soul's eye he found a light that transcended his mind. "It was superior because it made me, and I was inferior because I was made by it," he wrote.[18] He now saw God as Being—"You gave a shock to the weakness of my sight by the radiance of your rays, and I trembled with love and awe."[19]

The influence of Bishop Ambrose continued to stimulate Augustine's spiritual progress. Augustine wanted to know God, but he finally realized that this would not happen "until I embraced the mediator between God and man, the man Christ Jesus."[20] For a while he could only think of Jesus as "a man of excellent reason" and was not able to see him as "the Word became flesh" (John 1:14). His friend Alypius told him that Catholics believed that

Augustine

Christ was God clothed in flesh. Augustine knew that the Neoplatonists did not understand this, believing that flesh is inferior to spirit.

He then began to read the writings of Paul, where he found the truth of the Neoplatonists combined with the gift of God's grace. But much was lacking in the Neoplatonist understanding: tears of confession, a humble and contrite spirit, the guarantee of the Holy Spirit, the cup of redemption. They do not hear, "Come to me, you who labor." They do not learn from Christ because "he is meek and humble of heart."[21]

The well-known story of his conversion is found in Book VIII of *Confessions*. One day Augustine and his friend Alypius were visited by Ponticianus, an African who was surprised to find that Augustine had been reading the writings of Paul. He began to tell about Antony, an Egyptian monk who had gone out into the desert to live his Christian life. He added stories about other monks and monasteries, describing their simple lives of prayer and self-denial. This was all new to Augustine and Alypius. Augustine became agitated and said to Alypius, "What is wrong with us? What is it that you heard? Uneducated people are rising up and capturing heaven, and we with our high culture without any heart—see where we roll in the mud of flesh and blood. Is it because they are ahead of us that we are ashamed to follow?"[22]

He went out to the garden behind the house where he was living so he could be alone and face his inner struggle. He wanted to serve God but was neither willing nor unwilling. He was in conflict with himself. His old loves held him back. He recalled an earlier time when he had said to God, "Give me the gift of chastity, but not yet."[23] He feared that the prayer might be answered too soon. He was in anguish, not knowing what to do or which way to go in his quest for truth. He was deeply confused and needed to hear some word from someone that would calm him.

A word came. It was the voice of a child in a neighboring yard saying, "Pick up and read, pick up and read." He wondered

LONGING FOR GOD

if those words were used in a game, but decided they were a command from God. He returned to the house, opened Paul's letter to the Romans and his glance fell on 13:13–14, "Let us live honorably as in the day, not in reveling and drunkenness, not in debauchery and licentiousness, not in quarreling and jealousy. Instead, put on the Lord Jesus Christ, and make no provision for the flesh, to gratify its desires."

What did this mean to Augustine? Probably more than we can know. He learned that the key to overcoming his sexual passions was to "put on the Lord Jesus Christ." As Albert Schweitzer said, Jesus Christ is the key to the mystical life. Augustine had been reading Paul, and perhaps now he understood what Paul meant when he wrote, "If anyone is in Christ, there is a new creation: everything old has passed away" (2 Cor 5:17).

The words in Romans that he read in the midst of a crisis cut right to Augustine's heart. They described the life he had lived and what it would take for change. Sometimes people hear the right word at the right time; at a different time, it might not have had the same meaning. This was the right moment for Augustine. He did not need to read further, for he wrote, "It was as if a light of relief from all anxiety flooded into my heart. All the shadows of doubt were dispelled."[24]

His next act was to tell his mother, who received the news with joy. Monica, however, was in declining health. Suffering from a fever, she died at age 56. Augustine was 33. Remembering how ardently she wanted him to convert, he must have realized her frustration at seeing his life wasted. He was overcome with grief. Now was the time for a response. He was baptized along with his son, Adeodatus, and his friend Alypius, and soon returned to North Africa to establish a monastery at Tagaste with some friends.

During this contemplative time, Adeodatus died at a young age. That death, which filled Augustine with grief, seemed also to spur him to action. He was soon ordained and, within a few years, was elected bishop of Hippo, a post he would hold the rest of his life. He engaged in doctrinal disputes with the Donatists, who said that only people who had resisted persecution should be ordained, and Pelagianism, which advocated a degree of free will. The economy of North Africa had declined and his church was filled with people struggling to survive. He tried to give comfort and hope. Meanwhile, he wrote voluminously. Augustine died of natural causes in 430, while the Visigoths, one of the barbarian groups destroying the western Roman Empire, were invading North Africa. A year later, Hippo was evacuated and partially burned.

There has been an extensive debate about Augustine's mysticism, partly because of differing definitions of what mysticism is. There are two experiences reported in his *Confessions* that many consider mystical.

One was when Augustine was reading Neoplatonist writers who encouraged him to explore his inner self. While engaging in such introspection, he saw an unchanging light "higher than my mind."[25] He called it a different light from the kind of light we normally experience.

Upon reflection, he described a process of ascent similar to that of the Neoplatonists. He began with perceptions that come through our five senses: seeing, hearing, touching, tasting, smelling. That, he said, is as high as beasts are able to go. From there he moved on to reasoning, which takes us to intelligence. Then he withdrew from imaginative fantasies and was thereby freed to see the light. This led him to the conviction that the unchangeable is what really matters. He reported, "At that moment I saw your 'invisible nature understood through the things which are made'...Romans 1:20. In a flash of a trembling glance I attained to that which is."[26]

The experience was brief. "I crashed into inferior things," as human weakness made the experience unsustainable. The problem, he said, was his sexual habit. That was his main obstacle to the vision of God. His conversion, as we have seen, made it possible for him to live a celibate life: "You delivered me from the chain of sexual desire, by which I was tightly bound."[27]

The other, better-known experience, was with his mother at Ostia, described at the beginning of this chapter. He and his mother were living temporarily in a house in Ostia on the Tiber River. They had experienced a moment when they extended their reach and "in a flash of mental energy attained the eternal wisdom which abides in all things." "If only it could last," Augustine wrote.[28] We have already seen that one of the keys to the mystical life is the word of Jesus in the Sermon on the Mount, "Blessed are the pure in heart, for they will see God" (Matt 5:8). Augustine was painfully aware of his own impurity, which centered on sex. When his conversion made celibacy possible for him, a door was opened to a more mystical life.

Augustine's experience provides us with the insight that it is never too late to develop a profound spiritual life. The journey requires much patience, and the preparation may be a slow process. There are very few instant conversions. He had to recognize that the life he was leading obscured the truth for him. He wandered through Neoplatonism and Manichaeism. He probed Christian faith gently because of the influence of people he respected. He developed a great respect for a bishop, and he began to take instruction. But, for some reason, he was unable to break with his current life, even though he seemed very much to want that. He kept searching for the right intellectual and philosophical answers.

The key, according to *Confessions*, was hearing about people who had left the cities of the Roman Empire and fled to the desert to be alone with God. The discovery that they found God in simplicity rather than through intellectual curiosity pushed him to read the right biblical passage. Something clicked. Augustine realized that his effort had not accomplished what he wanted. It was not his own probing that changed his life forever, and it was a crisis of self-doubt that opened him to that incomparable gift of God's grace. God was already at work in Augustine's life, but it took him a long time to realize that.

We too must recognize that we will never find God by our own intelligence alone. Opening up to God, who is already in our life, means the surrendering of self, ego, false desires, and selfishness.

FURTHER READING

St. Augustine. *Confessions*. Translated by Henry Chadwick. Oxford World's Classics. New York: Oxford University Press, 1992.

Augustine of Hippo. *Selected Writings*. Translated by Mary T. Clark. The Classics of Western Spirituality. New York: Paulist Press, 1984.

Wills, Garry. *Saint Augustine*. Penguin *Lives*. New York: Penguin Putnam, 1999.

3

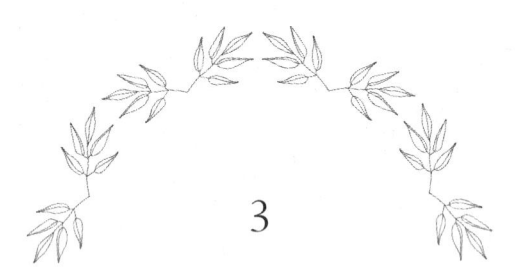

BERNARD OF CLAIRVAUX

1090–1153
A Powerful Leader and Quiet Mystic

It was cold at Clairvaux in the winter. The monks sat in their habits, covered by warm cowls with their hoods over their heads to find a little warmth. The stone monastery, built in its plain, early-Cistercian style with little decoration to minimize distractions and promote simplicity, was difficult to heat. The abbot had gathered the brothers together to begin explaining to them, in a series of sermons, the book that had guided his own spiritual development. He believed that a person could experience the presence of God. He was not a visionary, but sensed that a mystical experience was something interior. There was no sensory perception. Nothing was seen, heard, touched, smelled, or tasted, but it was nonetheless real, "when God himself is pleased to visit the soul that seeks him, provided it is committed to seeking him with all its desire and love." Desire is essential. "The fire of holy desire ought to precede his advent to every soul whom he will visit, to burn up the rust and bad habits and so prepare a place for the Lord."[1]

This was also a man of action, heavily involved in matters of church and state. He wrote letters to the kings of Europe and told them their duties. He settled ecclesiastical disputes between claimants for the papacy. He attended and influenced Church councils. He encouraged the second Crusade. Many scholars have described him as the most powerful man in Europe of his time.

This activity often took him away from the monastery. He missed it, and the monks missed him. Now he was back, ready to lead them through the spiritual struggles of the monastic life. They were eager to hear what he had to say. He told them that people in the world needed to be fed with milk, but the monks were going to get solid food, the bread of the subject. He had wisdom to offer those who had matured spiritually. The abbot was Bernard, and the scripture he would expound through eighty-six sermons was the Song of Songs, sermons that would constitute one of the great classics of Christian spirituality.

Bernard was born in 1090 in a small castle near Dijon into a deeply religious family. His father was a military man; his mother had connections with a number of aristocratic families in France. She died when Bernard was in his early teens; his father spent his last years in Bernard's monastery at Clairvaux. Bernard received a good education from the canons at St. Vorles in Châtillon-sur-Seine. He seemed adept at writing and had no interest in the popular sports of boys. He appeared to be indifferent to comfort as well as food and drink. He did have continuing health problems, particularly those associated with the stomach.

A young man with his education and talent would seem to have a bright future, but instead he chose the monastic life. He could have entered one of the grand and prestigious monasteries of the twelfth century, but around 1113 he entered the new monastery at Citeaux, known for its austerity and hard life, bringing with him, it was said, thirty of his friends and relatives.

LONGING FOR GOD

Stephen Harding, an Englishman, was abbot when Bernard arrived. The life was austere, the asceticism was very hard, the facilities primitive, and the land lonely. Only strong men could survive it. It was to this setting that Bernard arrived with his retinue. All four of his brothers would eventually become monks. He went through novice training and was soon sent from Citeaux to establish a monastery to be called Clairvaux. Starting a new monastery was not easy, and we know little of the work Bernard did in the beginning.

In 1125 he began to write. First is the *Apology*, in which he tried to calm controversies between Benedictines and Cistercians on the monastic life. Then came *The Steps of Humility and Pride*, as well as his popular *On Loving God*. Later he published a theological work, *On Grace and Free Will*. Around 1135–36, he began his best-known work, a series of eighty-six sermons on the Song of Songs, and only managed to get as far as chapter 3:1—"In my little bed I sought him whom my soul loves"—before he died, with Sermon 86 unfinished. His allegorical interpretation created a masterpiece of devotional literature.

Between 1130 and 1145, Bernard became deeply involved in affairs of church and state. He wrote letters to the kings and princes of Europe and told them their duty to their kingdoms and the Church. When two popes were elected by two different groups, Bernard worked to see Innocent II, a reformer, become the legitimate pope at the Second Lateran Council in 1139. In 1140, he succeeded in condemning Peter Abelard, a popular and controversial university professor, whose rational approach to theology conflicted with Bernard's contemplative mysticism. Whereas many theologians said, "I believe that I may understand," Abelard's approach was to understand before believing. Bernard influenced the choices of the bishops and abbots who were interested in reform. His most tragic effort was to support the Second Crusade, which turned out to be a disaster when the crusaders were defeated at Damascus in 1148, a defeat for which many blamed Bernard. In 1139, he was offered the archbishopric of Rheims, which he declined. In 1145, one of his monks became Pope Eugene III, marking the height of Bernard's power, after which he began to reduce his involvement in public life.

One of Bernard's most popular writings was a brief little book titled *On Loving God*. Emero Stiegman calls it an "epistolary tract." It was actually written for some Carthusians at the Grande Chartreuse in response to the question, "Why and how should God be loved?"[2] Bernard wrote that there are two reasons for loving God. First, "no one can be loved more righteously, and no one can be loved with greater benefit." But basically, he said, "I can see no other reason for loving him than himself."[3]

Further into the essay, Bernard outlined four degrees of love. The first is that we love ourselves for our own sake. Human selfishness is natural, but Jesus said that we are to love our neighbors as much as we love ourselves. However, love of neighbor should have its foundation in God. We cannot love others with purity if we do not love them in God.

The second degree of love is to love God for our own benefit, our own advantage. Bernard said we must learn that the benefits we enjoy are actually gifts of God's grace, not provided for our own merit.

This led to the third degree of love that is to love God for God's own sake. As we pray more frequently, our relationship becomes more intimate, which moves us to "taste and discover how sweet the Lord is."[4] Now our love becomes purer than does "the urgency of our own needs." This kind of pure love makes it more natural to love others.

The fourth degree of love may be the most difficult to understand, that we love ourselves for the sake of God. "Happy the man who has attained the fourth degree of love, he no longer even loves himself except for God."[5] When will we reach this degree of love? Bernard asked. Hence he began to describe the mystical: "To love yourself, as if you no longer existed, to cease completely to

LONGING FOR GOD

experience yourself, to reduce yourself to nothing is not a human sentiment but a divine experience."[6] It is necessary, he wrote, "that all human feelings melt in a mysterious way and flow into the will of God."[7] But when will this happen? Not until we are able to love God with all our heart, soul, and strength, he said. The ability to do this is a gift of God's grace. "It is in God's hands to give it to whom he wishes, it is not obtained by human effort."[8] Yet he also said we will more easily reach this highest degree of love when the desires of the flesh no longer hold us back.

Around 1135–36, Bernard began composing his sermons on the Song of Songs, a project that would continue the rest of his life. The medieval approach, as we saw in Origen, was to allegorize the Song. It was seen as an allegory of Christ, the Bridegroom, and the individual soul, or sometimes the Church as the Bride. The sermons represent Bernard's most mature thinking. Jean Leclercq, who edited the critical edition of Bernard's writings, described the series as "one of the greatest masterpieces of universal literature."[9]

Bernard began his sermons with the first line of the text, "Let him kiss me with the kiss of his mouth." That should get the attention of any audience. But this was not just the theme of the first sermon. Bernard wrote on that text for the first four and, after addressing a few other topics, went back to the kiss for four more sermons. What is the kiss of the mouth? It is the fulfillment of a desire uttered by a longing soul. It was not just a little peck or a formality of greeting, it was a kiss of the mouth, the kiss of lovers, the kiss of passion, the kiss of Christ, the kiss of a mystical encounter. "For," Bernard said, "this living and active word is to me a kiss…an unreserved infusion of joys, a revealing of mysteries, a marvelous and indistinguishable mingling of the divine light with the enlightened mind."[10] He was not interested in visions or dreams or figures of speech or parables. What Bernard wanted was the kiss of the mouth. That kiss is "the uniting of God with man."[11]

Where can we find the assurance that Christ the mediator

will never fail us? Bernard asked how he, who is only dust and ashes, can be sure that Christ will not revoke his word. His answer was, "Let him bend to me and kiss me with the kiss of his mouth."[12] Bernard ended this second sermon by telling the monks that the kiss was necessary for two reasons. First, without it, faith would not be strengthened. Second, the kiss is the mediator between oneself and God, Christ Jesus the Word.

He expressed a truth realized by most mystics. Anyone who has experienced "this mystical kiss from the mouth of Christ" is unable to describe it to anyone else. "Nobody can grasp what it is except the one who receives it." It is "hidden manna, a "sealed fountain."[13]

Bernard outlined a spiritual progression by using the image of a kiss. The first kiss is to kiss the feet of Christ and seek the forgiveness of sins. The second necessary step is the kiss of the hand of Christ, the hand that must lift us up and guide us in our spiritual growth. The third kiss is the kiss of Christ, holy intimacy that is "unbounded joy" in the presence of God.[14] These steps follow a well-known spiritual process: purgation, getting rid of sin so as to seek purity of heart; illumination, learning how to live the gospel in faith; and union, experiencing intimacy with God.

The desire to confess sin brings us to a sense of lowliness, of humility, before God. When we seek renewal and growth, we need the touch of God's hand. The experience of contemplation leads to ecstatic repose, which is the result of the kiss of Christ's mouth.

Having explained the images of feet, hands, and kiss in the first four sermons, Bernard picks back up on those images in Sermons 6, 7, and 8. So fundamental are these ideas that he could not let them go. The penitent's first kiss is to the spiritual feet of God. There are two feet, and Bernard labeled them mercy and judgment. When Bernard saw something numbered, he wanted to give those numbers meaning. These two feet, mercy and judgment, were the means by which Christ carried out his ministry.

LONGING FOR GOD

"Happy is the man then on whose soul the Lord Jesus once set these feet of his."[15]

How do we recognize a person who bears the imprint of the divine footsteps? The signs are mercy and fear. Fear is a sign of recognizing the judgment of God. The hope of forgiveness generates the sign of mercy. We must not kiss one without the other. Kissing only judgment brings despair; kissing only mercy generates a "pernicious security." The two must be kept in balance.

Sermon 7 addressed the kiss of the hand. Here he wrote about the two hands of Christ; one he called liberality, which gives generously, and the other, fortitude, which defends whatever it gives. Both of these hands must be kissed.

The kiss of the mouth was desired by the bride because she is "thirsting for God." A loving relationship is "the outstanding characteristic of the bride and groom," so the Song calls a soul that loves God as a bride. The person who asks for a kiss is in love. Love is fundamental to Bernard's spirituality. "Let him kiss me with the kiss of his mouth," is a spontaneous outburst. Would that all of Bernard's monks had that eagerness for God!

In this sermon he complained about those who went to sleep in the night office, the service of prayer. He quoted from the Book of Revelation, "Would that you were cold or hot. Because you are lukewarm, I will spew you out of my mouth (3:15–16)." The key for Bernard is upright intention to please God and to adhere to him. "This adherence to God is nothing less than that vision of God granted as a unique favor only to the pure in heart."[16] For this we cry out, "Let him kiss me with the kiss of his mouth."

In Sermon 8, Bernard added more meaning to the kiss. He referenced John 20:22, where the risen Christ breathed on his disciples and said, "Receive the Holy Spirit." That favor, said Bernard, was the kiss of the mouth. The Bride, in receiving the kiss, received the gift of the Holy Spirit. It is a twofold gift, "the light of knowledge and the fervor of devotion."[17] The Spirit, he said, "is fully equipped with the power both of kindling the light of knowledge and infusing the delicious nurture of grace." So, he wrote, the Bride who is about to receive the kiss must "set her two lips in readiness, her reason for the gift of insight, her will for that of wisdom, so that overflowing with joy in the fullness of this kiss," she may hear the words of Psalm 45, "Grace is poured upon your lips; therefore God has blessed you forever."[18]

While these sermons sometimes explode with the joy of mystical experiences, they sometimes reflect a more human side of Bernard. In Sermon 9, he wrote about his own mystical life. He is in love with God. He is thankful for the kisses of the feet and the hand. The favors he has received from God are more than what he deserved, but, he said, "They are less than what I long for." He cried out, "I ask, I crave, I implore; let him kiss me with the kiss of his mouth."[19]

In Sermon 14, he told the monks that in the early days of his conversion he "experienced coldness and hardness of heart" while at the same time he sought for the God he wanted to love. He already loved to some degree or he would not have sought God. But still he felt a wintry inward chill. However, there were unexpected occasions when God "set his wind blowing and the waters flowing."[20] Such occasions might be stimulated by the sight of a holy person, or the memory of someone once important to him. He was grateful, but concerned that it was memories of human good, not thoughts about God that stimulated his recovery. Still, he asked the question in Psalm 42:2, "When shall I come and behold the face of God?"

In Sermon 30, Bernard addressed a verse in the Song, "They made me keeper of the vineyards, but my own vineyard I have not kept" (Song 1:6). He is referring, of course, to Clairvaux—his own vineyard. There are many intruders. Little foxes destroy it (Song 2:15). There are "anxieties, suspicions, cares charge in from all sides; rare is the hour when bickering groups with their tiresome quarrels are missing from my door. I have no power

LONGING FOR GOD

to prevent them, no means of evading them, not even time for prayer." His vineyard is barren. It is gathered in bundles of twigs, "and consumed daily in your sacrifice by the burning fire of sorrow in my heart."[21]

He found another meaning for his monks in the passage "my vineyard I have not kept." Jesus said, "Those who lose their life for my sake will find it" (Matt 10:39). Peter and Paul were entrusted with many vineyards. For Peter it was the Jewish Christians; for Paul it was the Gentile Christians. They abandoned their own vineyards, their self-interests, in order to take care of these others because they were not afraid to die for "the name of our Lord Jesus Christ." Bernard confessed that he once lived at a lower level, looking after his own interests. But now he had different values. He identified with Paul's statement, "It is no longer I who live, but it is Christ who lives in me" (Gal 2:20).

Sermon 31 is built on the text, "Tell me, you whom my soul loves, where you pasture your flock" (Song 1:7). The woman wants to know where she can find her lover. Where can one find God? Bernard said that God is made known in a variety of ways because God cannot actually be seen yet. That is reserved for the next life. For now, God appears as God pleases, not as God actually is. "It is the form that seems good to him, not as he is."[22] What we see is what emanates from God, not God's self. Bernard cited Hebrews 1:1, "God spoke to our ancestors in many and various ways." One of these is seeing God "in the things that have been made." The created world is revelatory itself.

There is another way, divine contemplation, which takes place in the interior for one who seeks God with desire and love. Bernard quoted Psalm 97:3, "Fire goes before him and consumes his adversaries on every side." Holy desire is the fire that comes before the experience of God. This fire will consume "the rust of bad habits and so prepare a place for the Lord."[23] He quoted a series of texts to encourage the monks:

Bernard of Clairvaux

> Take delight in the LORD,
>   and he will give you the desires of your heart.
>   (Ps 37:4)
>
> Wait for the Lord and keep his way. (Ps 37:34)
>
> For there is still a vision for the appointed time....
> If it seems to tarry, wait for it;
>   it will surely come, it will not delay. (Hab 2:3)

He then turned to texts that are addressed to God:

> As a deer longs for flowing streams,
>   so my soul longs for you, O God. (Ps 42:1)
>
> Every day I call on you, O LORD. (Ps 88:9)
>
> Look down from heaven, and see. (Ps 80:14)

The Psalmist often expressed a deep longing for God, a desire to experience God on an intimate level.

In this sermon, Bernard described something of the nature of the mystical experience. The Bride wants to experience God inwardly. She wants to welcome God "into her inmost heart, into her deepest love; she wants to have the one she desires present to her not in bodily form but by inward infusion, not by appearing externally but by laying hold within. It is beyond question," Bernard wrote, "that the vision is all the more delightful the more inward it is, and not external." The senses play no part; nothing is seen, nothing is heard. The real pleasure in the experience is "the gift of love."[24]

Bernard's description of his own mystical experiences is in Sermon 74, written toward the end of his life.[25] He told the monks that the Word had come to him many times. Strangely, he said that he was never conscious of the time of the Word's coming.

LONGING FOR GOD

Sometimes he had a sense that it was coming, and later he remembered the experience, but he was never conscious of the Word's coming or going. He made clear that his senses were not involved. He did not see anything, there was no sound, no taste, no smell. He did not touch anything for "he is not tangible."

How did God enter Bernard's interior life? Perhaps, Bernard speculated, the Word did not enter at all because "he is not one of the things which exists outside us." But neither is he within, because the Word is good and Bernard modestly said that there is no good within him. Where is that Word that was made flesh and dwelt among us? "I have ascended to the highest in me, and look! The Word is towering above me. In my curiosity I have descended to explore my lowest depths, yet I found him even deeper. If I looked outside myself, I saw him stretching beyond the furthest I could see; and if I looked within, he was yet further within."

So, how did Bernard know that God was present? The answer is that the experience changed him and made him a better person. "As soon as he enters in, he awakens my slumbering soul; he stirs and soothes and pierces my heart, for before it was hard as stone, and diseased. So he has begun to pluck out and destroy, to build up and to plant, to water the dry places and illuminate the dark ones; to open what was closed and to warm what was cold; to make the crooked place straight and the rough places smooth, so that my soul may bless the Lord, and all that is within me may praise his holy name." For Bernard, what convinced him of God's presence was the movement of his heart. "I knew the power of his might because my faults were put to flight and my human yearnings brought into subjection." But, as all mystics know, the experience did not last. As a result, "all those spiritual powers become weak and faint and begin to grow cold." It was like removing the fire under a boiling pot. So, the words of Bernard are the words of the Bride, calling her lover back: "As long as I live, he wrote, the word 'return,' the word of recall for the recall of the Word, will be on my lips."

Sermon 84 opens with Song of Songs 3:1. "Upon my bed at night I sought him whom my soul loves." This is a sermon about seeking God. For Bernard, there was no greater good than to seek God. "The soul knows no greater blessing."[26] God is sought with the desire of the heart. Even when God is found, the soul continues searching because desire is kindled even more. And the reality is that the soul that seeks God has already been sought by God.

Bernard was concerned about his monks. "Many of you," he said, "walk in the love with which Christ loved us and seek him in simplicity of heart." However, there were some he was concerned about who had not shown any sign of receiving this grace because they only loved themselves. The verse "I sought him whom my soul loves," tells them what they should do, and that is to love God. "You would not seek him or love him," he told them, "unless you had first been sought and loved."[27] The reason for the search is love, and the fruit of the search is love. We could not love at all unless we have been loved.

Sermon 85 reopens the idea of spiritual marriage. "Happy the mind," he wrote, "which has clothed itself in the beauty of holiness and the brightness of innocence, by which it manifests its glorious likeness, not to the world but to the Word of whom we read that he is the brightness of eternal life, the splendor and image of the being of God."[28] The Word, of course, is the Word made flesh that dwelt among us (John 1:14). The soul that has reached this level begins to think of marriage. "Her declaration of love is a betrothal."[29] Bernard told the monks that when they see a soul leaving everything, clinging to the Word, living for it, and ruling her life by it, then they know that the soul is the bride and spouse of the Word.

The spiritual or mystical marriage gives birth to two kinds of offspring. The first "bring souls to birth" by preaching. The second "give birth to spiritual insights by meditation." In meditation one moves beyond bodily senses and loses awareness of the self. "This happens when the mind is enraptured by the unutterable

LONGING FOR GOD

sweetness of the Word, so that it withdraws, or rather is transported, and escapes from itself to enjoy the Word."[30] The first considers the needs of other people. The second "is allured by the sweetness of the Word." It is a good thing, Bernard said, to save souls, but being with the Word gives more pleasure. This "sweet intercourse" is a rare experience and, as he has said many times in the sermons, "lasts a short time."

In Sermon 86, the last, he continued his discussion of Song 3:1, "Upon my bed at night I sought him whom my soul loves." For Bernard, this is, among other things, a matter of privacy. He said that Christ encourages us to seek privacy when we pray in order to promote modesty. This launched him into instructions about prayer. We should pray in a time of leisure. Particularly suitable is a time when others are asleep and a deep silence is possible, when things are calm and free from noise. In prayer we must not seek anything other than the Word, "for in him are all things."[31]

In this final, though incomplete, sermon in the series, Bernard admonished his monks, "You will not pray aright, if in your prayers you seek anything but the Word, or seek him for the sake of anything but the Word; for in him are all things. In him is healing for your wounds, help in your need, restoration for your faults, resources for your further growth; in him is all that men should ask or desire, all they need that will profit them. There is no reason to ask anything else of the Word, for he is all."[32]

The sermon was never finished. He died in 1153 without completing the series. Others continued it, but no one could write like Bernard. For those who believe that these sermons are lacking in works of mercy and caring for the poor and suffering, it is important to remember that this mystic was also heavily involved in the affairs of the world in the twelfth century, advising kings and princes what to do, settling ecclesiastical disputes, administering a large community of men, and insisting that virtue was essential to the mystical life. He was away from his monastery for extended periods of time. He brought together the active and contemplative lives, demonstrating that you can have both in a well-developed Christian life.

For all of their imperfections, the monks were deeply loved by Bernard and they loved him. In a letter written to them while he was away, Bernard said, "My soul is sorrowful and will not be comforted until I return to you. Wherever I am your dear memory never leaves me."[33] In a letter to the Bishop of Lincoln, he wrote of Jerusalem, not the Jerusalem of the Near East, but "that free Jerusalem which is above and the mother of us all. And this," he said, "if you want to know, is Clairvaux. She is the Jerusalem united to the one in heaven by whole-hearted devotion, by conformity of life, and by spiritual affinity."[34]

The key elements for Bernard in finding God were desire and love. The intense desire of two lovers for each other as found in the Song of Songs was for him an image of our own longing for God. The kiss of lovers on the mouth represented the deepest intimacy with God. In his book *On Loving God*, Bernard takes us step-by-step through a process of developing an ever-deepening love for God.

Bernard is a classic example of a person who combined a deep inner life with service in the world. He traveled throughout Europe settling disputes and, in writing letters to the kings and princes of Europe, he reminded them of their duties to church and state, while at the same time living a mystical life. We do not necessarily have to give up our normal life in the world to develop a deeper inner life.

FURTHER READING

Bernard of Clairvaux. *Selected Works*. Translated by Gillian R. Evans. The Classics of Western Spirituality. New York: Paulist Press, 1987.

4

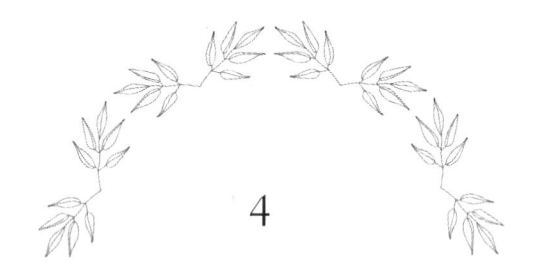

HILDEGARD OF BINGEN

1098–1179
Visionary, Healer, Artist, and Reformer

It was a dark, two-room hermitage, built of gray stone, attached to a Benedictine monastery, Disibodenberg. The monastery was founded in 1108 when the archbishop of Mainz summoned a group of Benedictine monks to establish this monastery. In keeping with the custom of the time, a small hermitage for a nun was part of the monastery complex. The monastery was located near the Rhine River, in the western part of the Holy Roman Empire, today's Germany. The first nun to live in that room was Jutta of Spanheim who, in 1106, chose the life of a recluse. Many communities in twelfth-century Germany had recluses in whom they took pride. Such women moved into a room in a church or monastery after which masons came and bricked up the outer doorway. These women lived lives of prayer and contemplation. Some offered spiritual direction, occasionally dispensing wisdom to those who would talk with them through a small window in an outside wall. A few were writers and others supported themselves as seamstresses. Still others, as Jutta, depended on the monks

Hildegard of Bingen

to bring her food and remove refuse. Jutta had a small opening through which she could observe Mass in the monastery and hear the Gregorian chant of the Divine Offices throughout the day.

Hildegard was sent to live in this room to lead this life at age eight. Born into a wealthy noble family with connections to political and ecclesiastical power, she was the youngest of ten children. Her parents, friends of Jutta's family, offered Hildegard to God as the hermit's companion and handmaid. Although her parents treated this as a pious deed, Hildegard never saw them again.

Jutta taught her to read the Bible in Latin and chant the Psalms of the Benedictine Divine Offices as part of their daily routine. The voices of two chanting women in a small confining room was a stark contrast to the deep booming voices of the monks. Following the schedule of the monks' liturgy gave structure to their day. Some believe that the monks taught her the Benedictine tradition and provided her with an intellectual education. Other women were attracted to Jutta's hermitage, and it eventually became a nunnery. As a teenager, Hildegard made a formal profession as a nun, and when Jutta died in 1136, Hildegard became the abbess of the women's community.

In the beginning of this book a statement was made that many mystics were skeptical of visions. Hildegard is included because she is one of the best known of the visionaries and there is considerable popular interest in her. Hildegard wrote that she had experienced visions since she was five years old. Chronic ill health, caused by a peculiar temperament, seemed to create an openness for such experiences. She claimed to see things others could not see, was able to perceive the future, and experienced what she called "the reflection of the living Light." On one occasion, while at prayer in the convent, she saw the Light itself, a direct experience of the presence of God.[1] She said that she could not describe it, but when she saw it, all sorrow and anguish left her, and she felt like "a simple girl instead of an old woman."

LONGING FOR GOD

One of her visions instructed her to move her community from St. Disibo, the male community to which her convent was attached, to a site near Bingen at an abandoned and ruined Carolingian monastery that she renamed Rupertsberg. She wanted to be free of the monks' supervision. Because of her growing fame, which brought public attention to the monastery, the abbot was opposed to the move and some of the nuns refused to go. One of the nuns to whom she was particularly close, Sister Richardis, left to become an abbess elsewhere, only to die a year later.

The move was made in 1150. The new place was in poor condition, but Hildegard remodeled and raised funds to stabilize it, and it began to flourish. By the 1170s, the house had places for fifty nuns, running water inside, and due to Hildegard's reputation, a constant stream of visitors. Here she would spend the rest of her life. Barbara J. Newman, a prominent historian of monasticism and spirituality, described her as "Benedictine to the core."

The monastic life was an option for a wealthy woman. The alternatives were an arranged marriage, about which she would have no say, or spinsterhood. Hildegard was criticized for only admitting the daughters of nobility to her monastery. On occasion she let her nuns wear jewelry since they were now free of domination by monks, who would insist that they wear veils. Elite abbesses tried to strike a balance between renunciation and privilege.

Hildegard wrote a brief commentary on the *Rule of St. Benedict*, by which monasteries were governed, visited a number of monasteries in an effort to settle their problems, and used moderation in what she demanded of her sisters. She believed she was called to be a prophet, and there is some controversy over whether she actually was a mystic. Scholars are divided. Some say yes, others no. She did claim to experience the presence of God, but unlike many mystics, she did not outline the steps to contemplation, nor was she the bride of the Song of Songs longing for union with God. She did not regard Christ as her lover.

Hildegard of Bingen

There was no sense of ecstasy. She never described her inner life until she was in her seventies.

Her secretary and first biographer, Guibert of Gembloux, asked her to tell him about her mystical experience. She responded with a letter. Her experience took place within her soul, which, she said, rose high into heaven. She saw a Light that was impossible to describe. It did not occupy space. She was able to remember the experience for a long time. Bernard McGinn wrote that the effect of seeing light suggests that she was having an immediate contact with God, the source of the Light. It would be difficult not to call her a mystic.[2] However, she stood between two worlds, the mystical and the prophetic, and the prophetic seemed to dominate. The prophetic visions she saw occurred while she was wide awake and alert, and there was no loss of consciousness. She was a reformer because of her visions. Others in this book were also reformers, such as Bernard of Clairvaux, Simone Weil, and Thomas Merton, but they did not claim visions to guide them.

In 1141, she reported seeing "a fiery light of exceeding brilliance." It penetrated both brain and heart and gave her instant knowledge of the Bible, justifying her ability to interpret it. This experience was a call to be a prophet in the tradition of the Old Testament. In her prophetic preaching, she criticized the neglect of Scripture, lukewarm and sluggish clergy, and the disregard of poorly informed laity. She saw her mission as doing what the clergy did not do: teach, preach, interpret the Bible, and proclaim the justice of God. She often used a disclaimer that she was just a woman in poor health and not educated, a line used by many medieval women writers who did not want men to feel threatened by their intelligence. Otherwise they might be in trouble with the Church.

Hildegard supported the reform movement initiated by Pope Gregory VII, who was concerned about the encroachment of the state on the Church. Kings and princes wanted to appoint

LONGING FOR GOD

bishops and other Church officials. She wanted the state to be subject to the Church, and was concerned about issues of clerical celibacy; simony, the buying and selling of Church offices; and the subservience of Church leaders to secular power. She did not preach about a second coming of Christ, but she did proclaim a coming judgment of God against the princes of the Church for their wealth, power, fornication, and negligence. The Assyrians were God's punishment on Israel, and secular powers would mete out God's punishment on the Church.

Hildegard was a prolific writer. She wrote on theology, medicine, natural science, and saints. Her correspondence included hundreds of letters. She even composed music. Her most important writing is popularly called *Scivias*, a shortened version of *Scito vias Domino*, which means "know the way of the Lord." Written between 1141 and 1151, the English translation in the Classics of Western Spirituality series by Paulist Press fills 469 pages.

In writing *Scivias,* Hildegard was assisted by a monk, Volmar, whom she loved very much, and by Sister Richardis von Stade, to whom she was very close. The book begins with a declaration that at age forty-three she saw a "great splendor" in which she heard a voice from heaven telling her to write. She was not to concern herself with rules of composition or the "understanding of human invention," but was to write what she saw and heard in "the heavenly places on the wonders of God."[3] She would not write by herself but by the will of God. What she saw was a "fiery light" that permeated her brain, heart, and breast. Immediately, she knew the meaning of the Bible—Psalms, Gospels, and other books of the Old and New Testaments. She did not see her visions in dreams, sleep, or delirium, or by her eyes or ears, but experienced them in her "inner self" while wide awake and alert. She heard a voice from heaven saying, "I am the Living Light, Who illuminates the darkness." She dated her writing by reporting that she wrote during the time of Henry, Archbishop of

Hildegard of Bingen

Mainz; Conrad, King of the Holy Roman Empire; Cuno, Abbot of Disibodenberg; and Pope Eugenius III.[4]

Scivias is a very complex book, filled with highly detailed visions and imaginative interpretations. Because of its length, just a few examples of the visions will have to suffice.

Book 1 opens with a vision in which Hildegard saw a mountain the color of iron on which God was enthroned, whose glory blinded her sight. At the foot of the mountain was an image with eyes on all sides in which she could see no human form. In front stood a child upon whom such glory descended from God that Hildegard could not look at the child's face. She discovered that the mountain had many windows in which appeared human heads. A voice cried out calling for her to speak of the origin of salvation and unlock the mysteries for people.

Hildegard's method was to describe a vision and then give an allegorical interpretation of it. The iron-colored mountain represented the strength and stability of the kingdom of God. The image with eyes on all sides was an allegory of people standing in the fear of the Lord. The child wearing a tunic of a subdued color and white shoes stood for the blessedness of poverty of spirit, which loves simplicity and sobriety of mind, following the footsteps of Christ. The heads looking out the windows of the mountain remind us that human acts cannot be hidden from God, but some do good works and watch with honor.

The second vision in book 1 involved seeing a great multitude of bright lamps that shone in fiery brilliance. A pit of great depth and breadth appeared emitting fiery smoke and a stench. This pit was hell. Within it were the breadth of vices and the depth of losses. The great mouth that emitted fiery smoke revealed souls that are sweet and gentle, but then deception led them into the torments of hell because they turned away from God when they despised the good.

Interestingly, Hildegard used this context to digress into a lengthy admonition on marriage. A man and a woman become

LONGING FOR GOD

one flesh in holy love "for the multiplication of the human race." They should never separate except for a reason that the Church allows, such as renouncing the world to contemplate Christ. They should not separate if only one partner wanted to do this. She added other rules. Blood relatives should not marry. A man who wanted to marry should be an adult and the woman of marriageable age. A man who had intercourse with a pregnant woman was a murderer. She also promoted chastity. Virginity, she wrote, "is the most beautiful fruit of all the fruits of the valley."[5]

One of the more remarkable visions in book 1 is vision 3 about the cosmos. The images of egg and globes, fire and winds, light and darkness, ether and water, are used to express human history, the coming of Christ, the Church, and things visible and eternal. In this vision she saw an egg-shaped "instrument" surrounded by fire and a shadowy zone under it. God used this fire to take vengeance on those who did not have the true faith, and to purify the faithful with the fire of his consolation. Within that fire was a globe of sparking flame held up by three little torches. The splendor of this sun's brightness revealed that within God the Father is "His ineffable Only-Begotten, the sun of justice" with his burning charity. Every creature was illumined by his light.

Sometimes this burning globe rose when the Holy Spirit brought celestial mysteries to pass in the Virgin Mary, through whom the incarnation came to the world. Sometimes the sun descended when the Son of God suffered misery and physical pain. After he showed his resurrected self, he returned to the Father. The fire that surrounded the egg-shaped instrument sent out blasts of whirlwinds where truth rushed forth and spread words of justice. But in the zone below the egg there was a horrible dark fire so terrible one could not look at it. The devil vomited out murder, which was full of avarice, drunkenness, and hardness of heart. This aroused the justice of heaven, which suppressed evil. Beneath this zone was the purest ether from which shone pure faith that depended on Christ. In this pure zone was a globe of fire—the moon—which was the "unconquered Church." This globe was held by two torches that represented the Old and New Testaments.

Book 2 on "The Redeemer and Redemption" opens with a vision calling Hildegard once more to her prophetic ministry. She described herself as "a person not glowing with the strength of strong lions or taught by their inspiration, but a tender and fragile rib imbued with a mystical breath."[6] She saw a blazing fire that symbolized the Omnipotent and Living God, whom she described as incomprehensible, undivided, inextinguishable, fullness, and wholly Life. God said to her that she was "wretched earth, untaught in all learning, and unable to read with philosophical understanding," but touched by "My Light;" she was to cry out and write God's mysteries she saw and heard in mystical visions.[7] This led to explanations by Hildegard of the incarnation, the Trinity, the Church, baptism and confirmation, religious orders and the priesthood, Christ's sacrifice, and the devil. This led to all sorts of rules and regulations. Men and women should not wear each other's clothes, women should not be priests, priests should not marry, people should not question transubstantiation (that bread and wine in the Mass change into the body and blood of Christ), and priests should use the proper vestments.

Book 3 is on "The History of Salvation," symbolized by a building. In the opening vision, Hildegard saw a block of stone, the color of iron, with a white cloud above it. Above the cloud was God seated on a throne, so bright that Hildegard could not see God clearly. God held to his breast a black and filthy substance surrounded by precious stones. From the throne of God there extended a great gold circle whose full width she could not grasp. It went from East to North to West to South and back to East, having no end. It shone with a "terrifying radiance the color of stone, steel, and fire" that extended from heaven to the abyss.

Out from God came a great star, and with it a multitude of sparks. These sparks first looked at God and then turned away, after which they were changed into black cinders and vanished. Then God admonished Hildegard to write what she saw and heard. God wanted her to speak about the Son of God, the intercessor, sent through the pure Virgin. Death was deceived without knowing it. The block of stone mentioned at the beginning of the vision revealed how firmly the fear of God must be held. Its breadth represented the incomprehensibility of God; its height was Divinity; its iron color meant that the fear of God was a heavy burden to carry and people rebelled against it.

The white cloud above the stone was human wisdom and the round throne above the cloud was the faith of Christians. Hildegard wrote, "Wherever the fear of the Lord takes root, human wisdom will also appear."[8] The black and filthy substance surrounded by precious stones that God held to his heart was humanity. God looked upon those who were saving themselves through penance. They were surrounded by jewels: martyrs and holy virgins and "penitent children of redemption." God knew, Hildegard said, that people will sin, but many will eventually be justified. God sent the Son, born of the Virgin, for the salvation of humanity.

Scivias ends with three final visions: The Last Days and the Fall of the Antichrist, The New Heaven and the New Earth, and Symphony of the Blessed. The first two of these visions sound much like the Book of Revelation in the New Testament. There are beasts, a youth in a purple tunic, a woman, a black and monstrous head, and a cloud covering a mountain. In the last days the Church will suffer terrible persecution. Faith wavers and scriptures are ignored. There are now new secrets and mystical truths that were hidden in books. God now warns the learned to proclaim the words that Hildegard has heard. The Antichrist will die and those who had erred will return to the Church, and there will be a new heaven and a new earth.

Scivias concludes with music composed by Hildegard praising Mary, patriarchs and prophets, apostles and martyrs, confessors

Hildegard of Bingen

and virgins. Finally, there is a brief morality play, the characters of which include virtues, souls, the devil, humility, and victory.

Hildegard was involved in many controversies. Emperor Frederick Barbarossa was her patron and supporter. In 1163, he granted her a charter of protection for her convent that granted certain liberties. He invited her to his palace to give a prophecy. However, their relationship changed when he began to support a series of antipopes, after which she referred to Frederick as a madman.

On another occasion, what Barbara Newman described as her "feisty and unyielding temper" brought down an interdict upon Rupertsberg. The issue was the burial of an excommunicated nobleman in her convent cemetery. She insisted that he had repented and died in a state of grace, but the Church authorities in Mainz insisted that his body be exhumed. Hildegard refused to obey, risking excommunication herself. The interdict meant that the sacraments could not be administered in Rupertsberg. She persisted, and the interdict was finally lifted just a few months before her death.

Why is Hildegard included in this book? She is very different from the other people studied here. She was, after all, a mystic by definition, one who had mystical encounters with God. The visions were out of the norm for many of the most best-known mystics. However, she is firmly situated in a tradition of visionaries. Among the women in that tradition are important people such as Elisabeth of Schönau, Marguerite d'Oingt, the aforementioned Julian of Norwich, and Margery Kempe.

What are we to make of this remarkable woman? How much did her poor health contribute to her visions? Did they have a physiological basis? Some in the medical community, including the popular Oliver Sacks, believed that she suffered from "scintillating scotoma," a form of migraine. Did this make her more receptive to God? We will probably never know. What we do know is

LONGING FOR GOD

that she wrote standard orthodox Catholic theology using imaginative allegory. *Scivias* is a complex book, not an easy read. Nevertheless, Hildegard was highly regarded in high places. Bernard of Clairvaux wrote to her, praising and encouraging her work. Replying to one of her letters, he congratulated her on receiving the grace of God and encouraged her to respond to it. He said he could not teach her anything because she had received hidden knowledge, and the anointing of Christ still lived in her. She had been able to discover the "secrets of heaven" and "things that are beyond the knowledge of man."[9]

Pope Eugenius III, encouraged by his former abbot, Bernard of Clairvaux, was impressed with *Scivias*. Securing a partial version, he formed a commission to study it. At the Synod of Trier, 1148–49, it received approval and the pope's endorsement. This increased Hildegard's confidence, but also increased her security against the biblical admonition that women were not to teach but must remain silent.

The early manuscripts of *Scivias* contained miniature paintings in color with gold and silver leaf. The artists are unknown and there is no evidence that Hildegard was a painter. A valuable Rupertsberg manuscript was destroyed in the bombing of Dresden in World War II. Fortunately, a photocopy had been made in 1927. From 1927 to 1933, a facsimile manuscript on parchment was made at Ebingen, a second monastery that Hildegard had founded, our only source of knowledge of the colors used in the miniatures.

The first printed edition of *Scivias* was done by a prominent Renaissance humanist, Jacques Lefèvre d'Etaples, in 1513. During the Reformation, Andreas Osiander wanted to see her as a Protestant because of her criticisms of the Catholic clergy. Later, there were efforts to attribute *Scivias* to Volmer or another male writer. The twentieth century saw a renewed interest in Hildegard, and current scholarship continues to seek understanding of this remarkable and complicated woman. No doubt there is more to be discovered and analyzed.

For now, what does Hildegard of Bingen teach us? Although she was a visionary, she insisted that such activity took place within her soul and she did not experience anything with her five senses. She saw a light, but it did not occupy space. These visions were part of her inner life, but they had relevance for her outer life. She was a reformer, and her visions led her to sense the incomprehensible nature of God. Light and fire were two of her most prominent images for God. Like many of the other people in this book, Hildegard tells us that God is a mystery; God simply cannot be defined. But she loved color and art and used it to express that mystery.

She insisted on right behavior on the part of Church officials, priests, and the laity because the lack of serious morality at all levels of society obscured the presence of God. Hildegard's insights call on us to examine our own moral lives as we continue the spiritual quest.

FURTHER READING

Hildegard of Bingen. *Scivias*. Translated by Mother Columba Hart and Jane Bishop. Classics of Western Spirituality. New York: Paulist Press, 1990.

5

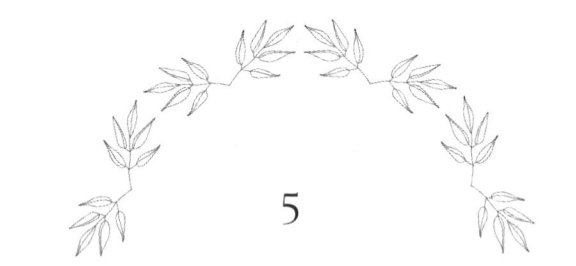

MEISTER ECKHART

ca. 1260–1327
Searching the Depths

He was standing nervously before a diocesan inquisitorial commission to defend himself against a charge of heresy. It was not uncommon for theologians to be questioned about their ideas, but this man's trial for heresy before the Inquisition was something new.[1] It was also dangerous. He had risen through the ranks of the Dominican order, and had recently moved to Cologne, one of the intellectual centers of his order. Fears of heresy were growing. The Brothers of the Free Spirit had been teaching that since they had had mystical encounters with God, they were no longer bound to moral teachings. That had poisoned the atmosphere for mysticism. The archbishop went after heresy wherever he suspected it. Our man was willing to renounce any errors in his preaching or writing, but that did not satisfy the inquisitors. The pope had appointed two commissions to investigate his ideas. This was a serious business. He wanted his case to be forwarded to Avignon, where the papacy now resided.

Accompanied by other members of his order, he began the long journey to France.

Meister Eckhart was one of the most influential and, at the same time, one of the most controversial mystics of the Middle Ages. The fourteenth century was noted for an intense mystical movement known as the Friends of God. Three examples of that movement are included in this book: Henry Suso, John of Ruusbroec, and Meister Eckhart. Eckhart is regarded by some as the father of that movement. Hence, he was known as "Master" Eckhart.

The movement was very informal. There was no organization or structure to it, but the members corresponded with each other. Some, like Eckhart, served as popular preachers and spiritual directors for people seeking a deeper transformation in God. Many of these mystics influenced by Eckhart have been rediscovered, and a considerable amount of scholarship is now devoted to their study.

We do not know an exact date for Eckhart's birth. He was German, and around the age of eighteen entered the Dominican order at the convent in Erfurt in the mid to late 1270s. The Dominican order was known for its intellectual emphasis and a commitment to orthodox doctrine. The *Constitutions* of the Order demanded the pursuit of learning. Dominicans were told to be unceasing in their learning so that night or day, at home or on the road, they should be reading and learning whatever they could by heart.

Eckhart's intellectual ability was noticed, and he was sent to the *studium generale* in Cologne to study theology and philosophy. Later, he studied in Paris while there was considerable controversy regarding those two fields. The question was whether philosophy should be used in the work of theology, or were they two completely unrelated fields? Eckhart believed, as did many Dominicans, that there was no contradiction between the two. Philosophy and theology fed each other.

LONGING FOR GOD

In 1294, he was called back to Erfurt, where he became the prior of the convent and an official in the order. As did most medieval writers, Eckhart wrote in Latin. However, wanting to influence more people, he began to write in popular German. His earliest work in that language was *The Talks of Instruction*, directed toward novices. While many medieval mystics were known for their rigorous asceticism, Eckhart was more interested in internal self-denial. One of his most persistent themes was detachment from things so that there would be no distractions to the search for God.

In 1302, he returned to Paris to teach theology. This represented the pinnacle of success for an academic. After two years there he was called back to Erfurt, where he was given a higher official position of provincial, or overseer, in the Dominican order for the province of Saxonia, which included forty-seven Dominican houses. During this time, he wrote *The Paradise of the Intelligent Soul*, in which he focused on the power of intellect over the will. The "temple of God" is the intellect. This is where God is to be found. The mystic soul loses itself in the Godhead, although God remains God and the soul remains soul.

Eckhart was successful in his work as a provincial, founding three new convents for women. In 1311, he was sent back to Paris for another two-year teaching term. Only one other theologian had ever done that: Thomas Aquinas, the most influential of all medieval theologians. After two years, Eckhart left Paris again and moved to Strasbourg, where he served as vicar to the Dominican Master General. Strasbourg had seven convents of Dominican nuns and a number of houses of Beguines.

Beguines were women who lived the monastic life, but took no vows, owned their own property, and were free to marry if they wished. Most lived in small communities, but some lived alone. The Church was always suspicious of them because their lack of formal structures made them difficult to control. Eckhart was influenced by these women, especially by *The Mirror of Simple*

Souls, written by Marguerite of Porete, who was burned at the stake for heresy in 1310, and Mechthild of Magdeburg's *The Flowing Light of the Godhead*.

Eckhart's *Talks of Instruction*, his earliest known German work, consists of twenty-two brief chapters. It is an account of the spiritual life as Eckhart understood it at that point in his life. It was probably written between 1295 and 1298 and was originally intended for Dominican novices, but since it was written in German it appealed to a broader audience. There are fifty-one manuscripts of this work that still exist, which indicates its popularity. There must have been many more in the thirteenth and fourteenth centuries.[2]

It begins with a discussion on obedience, which he called "a virtue above all virtues."[3] Everything is better when done under obedience, when our own will is not a factor. The best prayer we can pray does not ask anything for ourselves, but only that we receive what God wills. The most powerful form of prayer, he wrote, is that which comes from a free mind, a mind unencumbered with anything, that does not seek its own interests but immerses itself in God's will. The key is detachment. Eckhart urged his audience not to put too much importance on what they do but rather on who they are. Holiness is the result of the kind of people we are, not our actions. He urged his hearers to train themselves to keep God always present in their minds. Such people possess God wherever they are and with whomever they are.

One of the questions Eckhart asked, knowing that many people ask it, is what we should do when God seems absent and we are unable to find him. When we cannot find God, we should do what we did when we had previously found him. The basic problem is the desire to exercise our own will when the key is to seek what God's will is. Mary became the Mother of God when she gave up her own will. "Let it be with me according to your word" (Luke 1:38). The more we possess ourselves the less we are possessed by God.

LONGING FOR GOD

Several chapters in *The Talks of Instruction* contain discussions of repentance. True penance is not in doing ascetic practices such as fasting, keeping vigil, or going barefoot. True penance is turning away from all that is not God, raising the mind above all things into God. Sharing in the suffering of Christ causes sin to fall away from us. We should try to do all Christ did and refrain from what he did not do, always being mindful of him as he is of us. We should "grow up in every way into him" (Eph 4:15).

Near the end of the instructions, he described people who engage in great acts of asceticism and accomplish difficult and unusual works. They find great joy in these accomplishments that become a prop and support for their spiritual growth. Eckhart, however, said that God wants to take away these props. God's mercy and forgiveness are not given for such accomplishments; they are given because of who God is. God grants many gifts because of God's own goodness and does not want us to depend on props.

The key to understanding Eckhart is the illusive concept of the "ground." Eckhart said, "God's ground and my ground is the same ground."[4] The ground has been described as "the hidden depths of God" and "the innermost of the soul." These come together in the mystical experience of God. The Gospel of John expressed it when Jesus hoped that his disciples "may all be one. As you, Father are in me and I am in you, may they also be in us" (John 17:21). "In us" is a key mystical phrase. One scholar described the ground as "the identity of the divine ground with the ground of the soul."[5]

What a Christian seeks, according to Eckhart, is a kind of mystical unity that comes about in the unity of grounds, in which there is no difference between a human and God. That kind of unity is expressed in the Prologue to the Gospel of John: "The Word was with God, and the Word was God....And the Word became flesh and lived among us" (John 1:1, 14). So, the Word descended from God and we ascend by becoming one with

God. Since God took on human nature, all who possess a human nature can become one with God.

A dominant theme in Eckhart's mysticism is the birth of the Word in the human soul. He explained this in one of his most important sermons, designated by scholars as Sermon 101.[6] It appears to have been preached in the Christmas season early in the fourteenth century, the first in a series of four. As a trained scholastic theologian who hoped to relate faith and reason, he used a question-and-answer format. As the sermons progressed, the importance of reason diminished.

He based the sermon on a text from The Wisdom of Solomon, a book in the Apocrypha. "For while gentle silence enveloped all things, and night in its swift course was now half gone, your all-powerful word leaped from heaven, from the royal throne, into the midst of the land that was doomed" (Wis 18:14–15). At Christmastime, we sing about Christ being born in a silent night, but this sermon is about Christ being born in our souls, more specifically in our "ground." Meister Eckhart spoke of a good and perfected person—one who walked in the ways of God—experiencing this birth, while an undisciplined person would not know anything about it, let alone have the experience.

The first question: Where in the soul does God speak the Word? He answered that this birth will take place in the purest part of the soul, the ground, of one who lives in a noble way, is collected, and turns inward. It does not happen in the soul of one who uses the five senses to seek out many created things.

The second question: Should a person who seeks this birth of the Divine in the soul develop images of God and reflect on them? No, answered Eckhart. One should seek to be free of all thoughts, words, deeds, and images and keep a receptive attitude, letting God work within. This is apophatic theology, understanding God with no images, no concepts, no symbols. The opposite is cataphatic theology, which understands God as known through images and created things (see Rom 1:20).

LONGING FOR GOD

Another question: Where is the silence and the place where the Word is spoken? For Eckhart, it is in the soul's most secret part, the ground, called by some the spark of the soul. No creature can enter there and there is no activity or understanding in the ground. When the soul is free and has no images, God can freely unite with it. God does not need images, for God operates in the ground where no image or creature will ever find its way in. There must be stillness and silence so that God can give birth to his Son and do the divine work without any images. When we are young, we sometimes think of God as a grey-haired, old man in a white robe seated on a golden throne in a heaven surrounded by clouds, the "Ancient of Days" in the Book of Daniel. We may develop what we consider more mature images, perhaps something more nebulous but still located up in the sky somewhere. Our goal, however, should be silence with no images, and let God work in the ground. We live in darkness, God comes in darkness, but, as John put it, "The true light, which enlightens everyone, was coming into the world" (John 1:9). The Son came to reveal what was hidden.

Some mystics practiced a rigorous asceticism in an effort to purify themselves. They fasted, they went without sleep, they punished their bodies, they avoided heat in the winter. Eckhart, however, was more interested in self-denial in the soul: getting rid of images, ignoring knowledge that comes through the five senses, purifying our attitudes. It was these conditions, he taught, that enabled an awareness of God. This is knowing by not knowing, and it is this unknowing that draws us from all that is known.

Eckhart cited the disturbing words of Jesus in Matthew 10:37–38: "Whoever loves father or mother more than me is not worthy of me; and whoever loves son or daughter more than me is not worthy of me; and whoever does not take up the cross and follow me is not worthy of me." This meant giving up yourself and all created externals. Such a person, Eckhart believed, cannot be separated from God. In this context, he made a much misunderstood statement that such a person could not commit a mortal sin. This is the kind of statement that got Eckhart into trouble. The Brethren of the Free Spirit practiced a radical mysticism that taught they did not need normally accepted moral norms because they had attained union with God. That was not what Eckhart meant in that statement. He said that a person in whom Christ has been born in the soul would naturally do everything possible to avoid any sinful activity.

A general definition often used to describe late medieval German mysticism was "the transformation of consciousness through a direct encounter with God's presence."[7]

The second sermon in the series is built on Matthew 2:2, "Where is the child who has been born king of the Jews?" Eckhart's answer is it is in the ground, the essence of the soul. However, the powers of the soul can block reception of the Divine if it is absorbed in sin. Knowledge can also be a hindrance. Forgetting is more important than knowing, for this creates a clean, empty place for the birth to take place. The Word can only be heard in silence and stillness, passivity and reception.

The third sermon in the series is based on Luke 2:42–49, where Jesus went to the temple in Jerusalem at age twelve. His parents were frantic at not being able to find him. When they did, he asked them, "Did you not know that I must be in my Father's house?" So, to prepare for the eternal birth of Christ in the soul, we must leave the crowd as Mary and Joseph did and return to the ground, being passive and receptive.

Can we be aware of God's presence through our senses? Eckhart's answer is that God decides how he shows or hides himself. If the birth takes place, our response is to love God only. God waits for us with love.

In the final sermon in this series, the question is asked whether the eternal birth of Christ in the soul, the ground, happens continuously or only after great effort. Eckhart describes three modes of the intellect. First is the active intellect, which uses reason to bring people to God. Second is the passive intellect. When God acts one must be passive so God can enter the ground. Third is the potential intellect, which helps the soul prepare for a mystical encounter that may or may not happen. In this context, Eckhart discussed ecstasy or rapture as a characteristic of mystical experience. Such an event can only be brief "because of the strain it puts on the body; one can stand it only so long." The transfiguration of Jesus and the mystical experience of Paul were brief events. However, Eckhart, like many mystics, was suspicious. What one seeks is not an experience, but God.

Eckhart referenced Augustine in describing six stages of spiritual growth. Stage one of the growth of the inner person begins when one lives by the example of good and holy people, even though the individual is far from perfect. Stage two occurs when one begins to turn toward God and seeks divine wisdom. In stage three the person withdraws from the mother, leaving behind fear and care, and has no desire for doing wrong. Now one is constrained by love and a zeal for God. Stage four is when the person is more and more rooted in love and God to the point that he or she can endure opposition, temptation, and sorrow. Stage five involves living in peace and reposing silently in the gifts and wisdom of God. A person arrives at stage six when, free of all images, that one is transformed, experiences a complete oblivion of time, and becomes God's child. The final end of the inner person is eternal life. Then, Eckhart cited Augustine, "the image of God appears and shines."[8]

He preached to the people all over Germany and parts of Switzerland. Friars, nuns, beguines, and common folk listened to him eagerly, seeking that transformation that put them in touch with God. Eckhart lived the rest of his life as a vernacular preacher, encouraging detachment and mystical union with God. In late 1323 or early 1324, Eckhart moved from Strasbourg to Cologne, the intellectual center of Dominicans in Germany. His three years there were a time of controversy. Henry, the archbishop of

Meister Eckhart

Cologne, was a strong opponent of heresy and an ally of Pope John XXII in his conflict with the Emperor Louis of Bavaria. There was concern in the air about the Brethren of the Free Spirit and their belief that because they had mystical encounters with God, they could not commit any sin. In 1326, Eckhart appeared before a diocesan commission to defend himself against the charge of heresy. Eckhart said that he could be in error but not be a heretic, because error is a matter of the intellect, but heresy is a matter of the will.[9] The Church greatly feared heresy in the fourteenth century, and a mystic who wrote unusual ideas was a ready target. The particular concern was for uneducated people, who might not understand a mystic and be led into heresy.

Eckhart was concerned that the uneducated be educated, and, for that reason, he did much of his writing and preaching in German in the latter years of his life, rather than the customary Latin. In 1327, he was at the papal court in Avignon being tried for heresy and was ready to retract any error. Charges were investigated and 150 articles were ultimately reduced to twenty-eight. Eckhart denied that he had preached two of them. Some modern historians are now pointing out that many of the ideas of Eckhart that were condemned could have been found in the writings of the Church fathers, including his belief in the birth of the Word in the soul. It also appears that Eckhart did not put up a good defense. However, he was near the end of his life and would die the next year.[10]

The following year, a papal bull was issued listing the twenty-eight articles, seventeen of which were considered heretical, the others as containing "the mark of heresy." Since Eckhart was already dead, he was no longer a threat, and his followers believed Church authorities had misunderstood him. The pope finally absolved Eckhart of heresy, saying that at the end of his life he had professed the orthodox faith and "revoked and deplored the twenty-six articles which he had preached."

The cloud of heresy that hung over his thinking, however, did not diminish his popularity. People who knew him loved him

LONGING FOR GOD

and were grateful for his ministry. What he stood for was peoples' realization of their inner union with God.

The ground of the soul was Eckhart's most important teaching. It is a part of us untouched by anything other than God. When God's ground and our ground come together, the mystical life flourishes. Some interpreters have called it a spark or a divine flame representing divinity. It is for us to seek and nourish it as we probe the mystery of God. Eckhart taught the self-denial of the soul, freeing it of all images of God we have ever had. We know God by unknowing inadequate images and ideas of God. King Herod asked, "Where is the child who has been born King of the Jews?" The answer is that he is deep within us, in the depths of our souls. That is where we must look for God.

FURTHER READING

McGinn, Bernard. *The Mystical Thought of Meister Eckhart: The Man from Whom God Hid Nothing.* New York: Crossroad, 2001.

Meister Eckhart. *The Essential Sermons, Commentaries, Treatises, and Defense.* Translated by Edmund Colledge, OSA, and Bernard McGinn. The Classics of Western Spirituality. New edition. New York: Paulist Press, 1981.

Meister Eckhart. *Selected Writings.* Translated by Oliver Davies. Penguin Classics. New York: Penguin Books, 1994.

Meister Eckhart. *Teacher and Preacher.* Edited and translated by Bernard McGinn, with collaboration of Frank Tobin and Elvira Borgstadt. Classics of Western Spirituality. New York: Paulist Press, 1986.

6

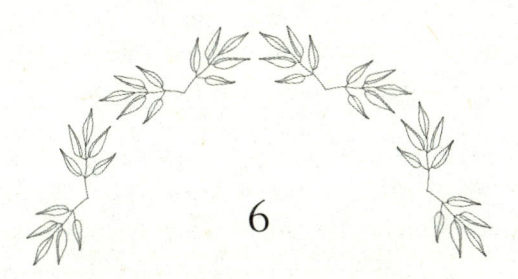

HENRY SUSO

ca. 1295–1366
From Self-Denial to Simplicity

Standing in the choir stall after the noonday meal, a melancholy friar felt himself strangely transported to another level of awareness, although he was not sure whether this was an in- or out-of-body experience. There was something of a vision, but it was without "form or mode." He did nothing but "stare into the brilliant reflection," unaware of himself and the passage of time. He could only describe it as "a sweet foretaste of heaven's unending bliss." He had no idea how long the experience lasted, but he hoped the memory of it would always stay with him. After this he went about his normal duties quietly and unnoticed, experiencing again "the bliss of God's touch" while seeming to walk on air.[1]

Henry Suso, born around 1295 in Constance, in the German part of the Holy Roman Empire, entered the Dominican order at age thirteen. He was obviously too young, but his parents had made a substantial gift to the order and it accepted him. Five years later he had this experience, which led him to a deeper religious life. In time he would become a part of the Friends of God

LONGING FOR GOD

mentioned in the previous chapter. Bernard McGinn wrote that Suso "is among the most influential, yet elusive, later medieval mystics," and added that "no fourteenth century mystic was more widely read and none more representative of the many strands of the mysticism of the century than this Dominican friar."[2]

His intellectual ability was recognized by his order, and he was sent to study philosophy and theology, first at Strasbourg and later at the *studium generale* in Cologne, the intellectual center of German Dominican life. In both places he would have met Meister Eckhart, who became a major influence on him although details of their relationship are "lacking."[3] No doubt he would have encouraged Suso in his mystical life.

Returning to his home convent, he was named a lector, or teacher, but because of proceedings of heresy against Eckhart and his use of Eckhart's ideas in his teaching, he was relieved of his position. Later, around 1329, while the controversy was still raging, Suso wrote *The Book of Truth* to defend Eckhart against his critics, although Eckhart had died by that time.

Suso and his Dominican brothers had to leave Constance because they supported Pope John XXII in a controversy with Louis the Bavarian, the Emperor. Louis opposed the tradition that the pope had to approve his election by the imperial electors before he could perform his duties. Louis wanted to be free of papal influence. The community moved to Dissenhofen in 1343, after which Suso began his career as an itinerant preacher and confessor, traveling about Germany and the Netherlands, presenting his mystical ideas. His primary theme was the inner transformation of the Christian. Around 1348, he transferred to the convent at Ulm, where he died in 1366.

There is an autobiography of Suso, *The Life of the Servant*, often regarded as the first autobiography in the German language, in this case Middle High German. There is considerable controversy about its origin. One of his spiritual directees, Elsbeth Stagel, wrote down notes about Suso's life from their conferences. When

Suso found out about them, he took them back and began to burn them. In the midst of this destruction, something led him to believe that God wanted him to stop, which he did. The autobiography is based on the remaining notes plus items added by Suso "by way of good instruction." Suso eventually prepared a collection of his writings titled *The Exemplar*, for which he might have done more editing of his *Life*.

In his early years in the convent, Suso said that he was irritated by many temptations. Hoping to deal with them by asceticism, he went back and forth on what he should give up. Friends warned him about "exaggerated efforts," and counseled moderation, a virtue that was foreign to Suso. He recognized that to possess the world yet serve God perfectly was attempting the impossible. One cannot serve two masters.

The next stage in his growth was spiritual marriage to Eternal Wisdom, described in chapter 3 of his autobiography. Eternal Wisdom is Suso's metaphor for God. It is a very complex metaphor. Although he often saw Eternal Wisdom as a woman, a beautiful maiden, a wise mistress, a queen, at other times she became a noble youth. Suso also wrote about Eternal Wisdom taking on the flesh of a male human, Jesus Christ. Bernard McGinn called this "gender bending."[4] He noted that God is without gender, but Christians usually refer to the first two persons of the Trinity as male, and some mystics have described their experience with God as a feminine soul in love with a man. Shifting gender identities was not uncommon in the writings of mystics.

Once again, we face the problem of a lack of language to describe a mystical life. Allegory and analogy are the only resources available. While we are stuck in the reality of genders, the mystics had no problem in confusing them. The soul is often designated by feminine terminology, and God is almost always described as male. These designations do not always work in trying to describe the mystical life, so mystics do the best they can by using male and female in ways that best described what has

LONGING FOR GOD

happened to them. Is Wisdom male or female? Can a man have a feminine soul? Mystics use what works for them in a particular situation.

Suso also used the language of medieval courtly love. Troubadours often sang of their beloved as someone they loved but whose presence they could never approach. About Eternal Wisdom Suso wrote, "O God, if I could catch one glimpse of her, speak to her for a few moments." He asked, "Is this loved one God or human, man or woman, knowledge or wisdom? Or what else can it be?"[5] Romantic love is often used as an allegory for loving God and the Song of Songs is frequently interpreted this way.

While pondering these questions, Suso had another experience in which he saw Eternal Wisdom as a woman high above him on a throne of clouds. "She shone as the morning star and dazzled as the glittering sun. Her crown was eternity, her attire blessedness, her words sweetness, and her embrace the surcease of all desire." He sensed her as distant, yet close; above, yet low; present, yet hidden. "She towered above the summit of heaven and touched the bottom of the abyss." Eternal Wisdom said to him, "Give me your heart," to which Suso replied, "You are now the empress of my heart and bestower of all graces. I have riches enough. I no longer want anything the world has to offer."[6] He added that as soon as he thought of her as a "beautiful young lady," he suddenly found a "proud man before him."

Sorting out this kind of language is a challenge. Suso did not find it easy to come up with adequate terminology to describe his experience. He used a sequence of opposites: far above, yet low; present, yet hidden; heaven and the abyss; beautiful lady, proud man. Something indescribable happened within him; he was at a loss to explain it. He had an encounter with transcendence, and it changed his life.

Mystics know that purity of heart is the key to knowing God, but how does one achieve that kind of purity? Suso is an

Henry Suso

extreme example in the way he used ascetism in an attempt to achieve that purity.

The beginning of this is described in his autobiography. He carved the monogram of Christ, IHS, in his flesh right over his heart.[7] He told about an undergarment he wore that had 150 brass nails turned toward his body. He wore leather gloves at night that had brass tacks that would prevent him from removing the undergarment at night. He slept with a belt around his neck to which his hands were fastened. Finally, after sixteen years of this he had a vision of a heavenly gathering in which God told him to stop. He threw these garments into a river.[8]

But later he developed other ascetic practices. In order to show his compassion for the crucified Christ, he wore a cross on his back with thirty nails in it in an effort to praise Christ and identify with his suffering. He pressed the cross to his back so the nails would wound him and took the discipline, which meant whipping himself when he contemplated the crucifixion. On one occasion, he held the hands of two girls while they sat next to him in church. He regretted it so much that he went to a private place and threw himself on his back where his cross was fastened.[9]

Did these things actually happen? Rufus Jones, the Quaker historian of mysticism in the first half of the twentieth century, had doubts. "I do not trust the written account of his inhumanities to himself as a literal narrative."[10] Bernard McGinn also had questions. He said it is certainly possible that Suso engaged in such severe asceticism, but he thinks it unlikely, and in some cases impossible. What mattered was the exemplary nature of these stories, not their historicity.[11] Finally, sometime in the 1330s, Suso abandoned all excessive asceticism. He had a sense that new sufferings would come in a different form.

Suso's mentor, Meister Eckhart, said that interior asceticism was more important than just physical self-denial. Many religious people struggle with how to eliminate distractions. Mental distractions, when it is difficult to focus attention and stop distracting

LONGING FOR GOD

thoughts flowing through the mind, require much more effort to control than efforts to control the body. Suso finally realized that. Having spent most of his religious life wrestling with interior issues and having numerous mystical visions, Suso now devoted himself externally to work for the salvation of others. His main focus became the inner transformation of the person.

The Life is filled with descriptions of many mystical experiences. He tells us that one morning as he noticed the rising of the morning star, he heard a voice singing, "Mary the Star of the Sea has risen." It produced, Suso said, "a supernatural surge within him," and he began to sing along with the voice. Then he felt an "indescribable embrace" and heard the words, "The more lovingly you embrace me and kiss me in the spiritual manner, the more lovingly and affectionately shall you be embraced in my eternal splendor." There followed a series of experiences, one with a "heavenly youth," one with an angel who taught him how to look within his soul and see Eternal Wisdom "sitting quietly with a pleasing appearance," and another with a young man who said he came from God to give Suso "heavenly joys in his suffering."[12] In chapter 6, he tells about how souls of the dead would appear to him. One was the soul of Meister Eckhart, "clothed in ineffable glory, wholly deified in God." He told Suso to "withdraw from himself in deep detachment and receive all things from God and not from creatures."[13]

Suso's mystical doctrine is described in Chapters 46–53 of his *Life*. A continuing issue in the mystical life is the place of reason. Scholastic theologians had been trying to demonstrate by the use of reason that Christian doctrine was rational and logical. Many mystics found no place for reason in the spiritual quest. A mystic must transcend the limitations of human reason. Suso condemned unreasonable people who judge by human standards and show no connection between inner belief about outward conduct. However, Suso praised inward reasoning because "reason, being God-like, illustrates man's mental faculties as the stars glitter in the night sky." He added that reasonable doctrine detaches a person from sensuality and directs one "on the right way of reasonable truth."[14]

Suso discussed three kinds of withdrawal. First, there is complete withdrawal, such as when a thing ceases to exist. The rational soul, however, will always exist. It has godlike intellectual powers because the soul has been formed by God, who is "an intelligence above being."

A second kind of withdrawal is what he called a half-withdrawal, such as Paul's conversion experience when he is "transported in contemplation to the naked Godhead." However, when the experience ended, Paul was the same person he had always been.

The third kind of withdrawal is what Suso called "borrowed withdrawal," when a person gives up free will and surrenders the self to God in every moment. But this cannot be permanent since body and soul are together. One returns to one's former self and this withdrawal must be repeated again and again.[15]

Chapter 49 is a six-page list of inward behaviors a Christian should practice. Most of these are one-sentence statements. These are a few, for example:

- Keep your conduct discreet and do not be impetuous in word and deed.
- He who forsakes himself with respect to impulsive desires of the senses has achieved conquest of the self.
- A humble and restrained manner of conduct is proper for you.
- Strive to give your reason prominence in your actions because all evil comes from the overhasty impulsiveness of the senses.

LONGING FOR GOD

- A detached person must be freed from the form of creatures, formed with Christ, and transformed in the Godhead.
- A detached person should not constantly be looking to see what he needs. He should look to see what he can do without.[16]

In the final chapters of *The Life*, Elsbeth Stagel asked him a series of theological questions to which he gave extended answers. A basic question was, "Tell me what God is or where he is or how does he exist? That is to say, how is he one and yet three?"

Suso responded that the great theologians have never been able to explain this completely because God is above all thought and intellect. Yet, it is possible to have some knowledge of God by "studiously searching." For Suso, "Knowing God is a person's highest beatitude." He described God as "Eternal, without before and after, he is one, immutable, noncorporeal, essential Spirit. His essence is his life and activity. He is supernatural, unspeakable, blissful beatitude to himself and to all those destined to share that bliss with him in contemplation."[17]

Stagel asked, "Where is God?" Suso answered the question by referencing the theologians who say that God does not have a where because God is present in everything. He used a sentence often found in medieval literature, "God is like a circle whose center is everywhere and whose circumference is nowhere."

Suso believed that we come from God and return to God. This is part of the meaning of the Trinity for him. "The Masters tell us that in the outpouring of the creatures from their first origin there is a circular return from the end back to the beginning." In trying to explain the Trinity to Stagel he said, "No one can fully explain how the Three Persons can exist in the unity of essence."[18]

In chapter 52, Stagel wanted to know "how a soul experienced in mystical ways reached its supreme goal." Suso quoted John 12:26, "Whoever serves me must follow me, and where I am, there will my servant be." Whoever followed Christ to the crucifixion and shared in that shame would receive Christ's promise to share with his friends the exhilaration of his "naked God-sonship" in both time and eternity. This was to be found "in the marvelous brightness of the divine unity."

Then Suso changed the image from brightness to the darkness of unknowing, where multiplicity disappears and one loses one's individuality. "To have lost oneself herein perpetually is eternal blessedness."[19] Suso correctly wrote, "It is with great difficulty that the spirit of man grasps what has been said thus far."

After the soul has been stripped of its own will, it merges into the naked Godhead—pure being—not mixed with anything human. Suso referred to the "incomprehensible comprehensibility" of the three divine persons of the Trinity, which is pure being and the source of all being. The soul is suspended in the "divine Nothingness of God's incomprehensible wisdom" that causes it to forget all creatures, but at the same time not destroying its own comprehension. He told Stagel, "Mystic union is that point where the soul arrives at abandonment of self and all creatures in the naked Nothingness of the Godhead."[20]

Suso used difficult language here. Why did he write about the Nothingness of God? It is because God is not a thing; God is Being. As God said to Moses, "I AM WHO I AM....You shall say to the Israelites, 'I AM has sent me to you'" (Exod 3:14). We cannot see God because there is nothing to see. God is pure Being. The most basic theological statement we can make is, "God is."

He concluded chapter 52 of his *Life* with what is obviously a speculative account of the soul's encounter with God. In a mystical experience, the soul senses a "refining light" from the Godhead that purifies the soul. It loses any awareness of itself, its individuality. In a sense it has lost its own being and found the Supreme Being. The soul experiences "exhilarating bliss."

Elsbeth Stagel exclaims, "Ah, how wonderful. How can a person arrive there?" Suso said it involves trudging "resolutely

LONGING FOR GOD

uphill," getting rid of all interior and exterior concerns and whatever interests us. We continue to plod along until the mind is "stripped of all knowledge." Since God cannot be known by human science or by images, we must think of God in a negative way, recognizing that any image is inadequate. "Here," Suso wrote, "every cord must be snapped and all creatures abandoned." In this darkness there is a "scintillating radiance, illuminating all things." The intellect is flooded with new knowledge and "the soul experiences ever new and ever changeless wonders."[21]

Suso struggled with language, trying to find words and images to describe the indescribable. For him, God was a "dark stillness, a hidden mystery." Based on his experience there is truth here, but these words are not to be taken literally. There are no words available to describe a mystical encounter with God, so these writers do the best they can to give us some sense of their experience.

Suso's *Life* is his most read book today, but another of his books, *Clock*, a Latin version of his German *Little Book of Eternal Wisdom*, was very popular in the late middle ages, second only to *The Imitation of Christ*, usually attributed to Thomas á Kempis. The *Little Book of Eternal Wisdom* is divided unevenly into three parts. Part 1, the first twenty chapters, focuses on the passion of Christ. Part 2 has four chapters dealing with death, inward living, how to receive God, and perpetual praise. Part 1 lists one hundred meditations on the crucifixion of Christ. There are more extant manuscripts of this book than any other German book, which attests to its popularity. Most of it is presented as a dialogue between Suso, designated as "The Servitor," and Eternal Wisdom.

One matter that concerned Suso deeply was the alternation of the presence and absence of God. Sometimes God is clearly present to him; other times he experienced only the pain of God's absence. Eternal Wisdom described the game of love. Lovers appreciate each other more when they are apart than when they are together. Absence creates a longing for the other. Suso called this "a tiresome game" and said, "O Lord, waiting a long time is painful."[22]

Chapter 22 contains instructions from Eternal Wisdom on how to live interiorly. There were four important points:[23]

1. Keep detached from others.
2. Disengage from all outside images.
3. Avoid anything that would bring disturbance, detachment, and struggle.
4. Elevate the mind in the contemplation of God.

Henry Suso went through many stages in his life, from obtaining a scholastic education, to observing severe asceticism, to leading his life as a teacher, spiritual director, preacher, and writer. He was a visionary mystic and one who sought inner transformation for himself and for others. So doing, Suso taught us that excessive self-denial is not the solution to our quest for God. He concluded what many other mystics said, that true asceticism is not physical, it is interior—in the heart. Purity of heart is more important than purity of the flesh. Later in life, Suso's focus on transformation of the inner person involved moving beyond the limitations of reason and freeing oneself from images of God that are always inadequate.

FURTHER READING

Suso, Henry. *The Exemplar: Life and Writings of Blessed Henry Suso, OP*. Translated by Sister M. Ann Edward, OP. 2 vols. Dubuque, Iowa: Priory Press, 1962.

———. *The Exemplar, with Two German Sermons*. Translated and edited by Frank Tobin. The Classics of Western Spirituality. New York: Paulist Press, 1989.

7

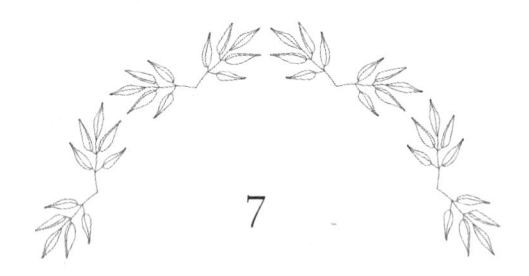

JOHN OF RUUSBROEC

1291–1381
Craving for God

He sat quietly in the woods of Groenendaal with his wax tablet and stylus, writing a treatise on how a new community of Poor Clares—a women's Franciscan order—should live their lives in a convent. He loved the solitude of the woods with the tall trees, the leaf covered ground, and the sounds of birds singing and animals scampering across, around and up and down the trees. Here he could meditate and write alone but would have to return to the community at the end of the day. Groenendaal was a house of hermits who longed for a life relatively free of the distractions of the city, where they could focus on their mystical lives.

His name was John of Ruusbroec, one of the great mystics of the Church. He was born in 1293 in a small village a few miles south of Brussels. At age eleven he was sent to Brussels to be educated by an uncle who was a priest. He was ordained at age twenty-four, a year earlier than normal, and spent the next twenty-six years as an assistant pastor in the church of St. Gudula

John of Ruusbroec

in Brussels, where his uncle was a canon. In 1343, Ruusbroec, together with his uncle and another canon, moved to an old hermitage at Groenendaal (Green Dale) and began a community of hermits that would adopt the Rule of St. Augustine. Ruusbroec became the prior and spent the last thirty-eight years of his life there.

Why did these men move to rural Gronendaal? They believed that the city was too infused with materialistic values. Continuing construction at St. Gudula's was noisy and distracting, and it was impossible to develop a deep spiritual life there. These were uncertain times in the Church. The papacy had moved from Rome to Avignon, France, and there rose up a host of extremist movements: Franciscan Spirituals, Beghards, reborn Waldensians, and heated disputes flared up everywhere. War and plague added to the uncertainty. Since the hermitage provided a much better environment for the flourishing of a deep spiritual life, others joined as well, and Groenendaal became a place of pilgrimage.

A biography of Ruusbroec by Henry Pomerius, written some forty years after his death, noted that visitors from all over Europe came to Groenendaal to consult with Ruusbroec. Among those pilgrims was Geert Groote, a founder of the Brothers of the Common Life, which gave us one of the most widely read medieval books, *The Imitation of Christ*, usually attributed to Thomas à Kempis.

During his life, Ruusbroec wrote eleven books. Five were written during his years as a priest in Brussels. His first, dated around 1130, was *The Kingdom of Lovers*, an effort to explain union with God through the seven gifts of the Holy Spirit. He later regarded this book as immature and did not want it copied. It was, however, and the Carthusians of Herne had the illicit copy. Consequently, Ruusbroec wrote for them *The Book of Clarification*, in an attempt to explain it. One of Ruusbroec's primary themes was union with God through the practice of virtues. The

LONGING FOR GOD

Spiritual Espousals, arguably his most important work, is a more thorough explanation of his mystical theology. It is based on Matthew 25:6, "Look! Here is the bridegroom! Come out to meet him." A more concise summary of his thought is *The Sparkling Stone*, the most accessible of all of Ruusbroec's writings. *The Four Tempations* (concupiscence, pride, learning, and indolence) was written for the Beguines. *The Christian Faith* was a catechetical work.

He began writing *The Spiritual Tabernacle* in Brussels, but completed it at Groenendaal. There he also wrote *The Seven Enclosures*, mentioned above, for Margaret of Meerbeke of the Poor Clares. *The Mirror of Eternal Blessedness* was concerned with the Eucharist and is sometimes called *The Blessed Sacrament*. It also attacked a men's group, the Brothers of the Free Spirit, who believed that because they had perfect union with God, the usual moral norms did not apply to them. They could do whatever they wanted and were often accused of sexual misconduct. *The Twelve Beguines* was his final work, a collection of treatises. All of his books were written in Flemish and were soon translated into German.

Thomas Merton, an American twentieth-century mystic, knew about Ruusbroec. In his *Sign of Jonas*, he reported that his confessor had told him, "I ought to pray to understand writers like Ruusbroec and go on reading him." Later, Merton wrote, "The garden [at his monastery] was like Eden and I walked there reading Ruusbroec." A fourteenth-century mystic was still relevant in the twentieth century as a guide for the spiritual life.[1]

Ruusbroec was one who carefully outlined his ideas: three things that make a good person, three things that a spiritual person needs, three things a contemplative needs, five kinds of sinners that ignore God's call, four ways of experiencing union with God, three stages of the spiritual life, three modes of meeting God without intermediary, three deviations from these modes, and on and on.

John of Ruusbroec

The Spiritual Espousals is a lengthy text, explaining his ideas about the mystical life in a thorough and comprehensive manner. It is based on Matthew 25:6, "See, the bridegroom is coming. Go out to meet him."[2] The bridegroom, of course, is Christ, and we are called to go out and meet him. That is what the contemplative life is all about, encountering the Divine.

The book is divided into three sections. Book One: The Active Life; Book Two: The Interior Life; and Book Three: The Contemplative Life.

"The bridegroom is coming." How does Christ come to us? Ruusbroec described three ways. First, Christ comes into our hearts. He comes in the form of an inner impulse of the Holy Spirit that encourages us to virtue. This generates heat in our hearts, for "the Spirit of God enkindles his fire in our hearts."[3]

The second coming occurs in the three parts of the soul. Ruusbroec used Augustine's description of the soul consisting of memory, intellect, and will. We are to fix our memory on bareness, freeing ourselves from all sensory images and multiplicity. The use of interior affection and love, as well as knowing God's faithfulness, makes us aware of Christ coming into our intellects, which brings us some level of enlightenment. Christ's coming into our will enkindles a fire, which generates a spiritual love that is beyond effort.

He summed up this coming of Christ in the soul through three streams. Through the first stream, memory is raised above sense impressions. Through the second stream, reason and understanding are enlightened to be able to know the virtues and mysteries of Scripture. Through the third stream, the will is set aflame in a quiet love endowed with great spiritual riches.

The third coming is into our spirit, beyond our ability to comprehend and understand. God's grace flows into our spirit and urges us on. It wells up like "a living, welling vein out of the living ground of God's richness, and one feels the touch of God's richness." One experiences this touch passively, "for here there is

LONGING FOR GOD

a union of the higher powers in the unity of the spirit, and at this level no one is active but God alone.[4]

The last section of *The Spiritual Espousals* focused on, "to meet him" from Matthew 25:6. "The Bridegroom is coming. Go out to meet him." What does this mean? For Ruusbroec it meant a person "transcends his creaturely state and finds and savors the riches and delight which God is himself and which he causes ceaselessly to flow forth from the hidden depths of the spirit."[5]

The meeting of the person and the Divine is a meeting in love. Ruusbroec wrote, "It is in this more than anything else that our highest blessedness resides." Here we encounter "the rich embrace of the essential Unity in this abyss of the ineffable." What fervent interior spirits seek is "that dark stillness in which all lovers lose their way." His closing benediction in the book is, "may the divine love grant us this, for it turns no beggar away."[6] Once again, as we have seen in so many mystics, the whole point is a matter of being lost in the mystery of God by probing our spiritual interior.

The Sparkling Stone provides a briefer, basic summary of Ruusbroec's thought and is a good entry point into his mystical theology. Early in this treatise he outlined four qualities that lead to perfection: (1) being zealous and good, (2) being interiorly fervent and spiritual, (3) being lifted up to the contemplation of God, and (4) going forth to all persons in common. When all four of these are found in one person, that individual has reached perfection. One will grow in grace, in virtue, and in the knowledge of truth.[7]

Ruusbroec defined a good person as one who has a purified conscience, is obedient to God and the Church, and intends God's glory in everything he does. The spiritual person is one whose heart is unencumbered with images, who has spiritual freedom in his desires, and has experienced union with God. The one who cleaves to God is free from images. By "spiritual freedom in his desires," Ruusbroec meant one who renounces

John of Ruusbroec

"fleshly affection." Images, such as Christ's passion, are useful in devotion, but one who seeks God must descend ultimately to an imageless barrenness.

The contemplative person places his or her entire life "on the foundation of a groundless abyss." Contrary to Meister Eckhart, Ruusbroec said that union with God has no ground. It is "infinitely deep, infinitely high, and infinitely long and wide."[8] We must, he said, "place our entire life on the foundation of a groundless abyss," that is, plunge ourselves into love and immerse ourselves in a depth that has no ground. Then we will be able to ascend to God, transcending ourselves, where "we will also melt and be dissolved, revolve and be eternally whirled around in the maelstrom of God's glory."[9] That is a powerful image!

My favorite quotation from this book is one I have often used in leading retreats in the hope of stimulating an interest in contemplation:

> A contemplative who has renounced himself and all things…can constantly enter the inmost part of his spirit in a state of barrenness and freedom from images. There an eternal light is revealed to him, and in this light he experiences the eternal call of God's Unity. He also feels himself to be an eternal fire of love, which desires above all else to be one with God. The more he perceives this attraction and call, the more he feels it, the more he feels it the more he desires to be one with God.[10]

God, said Ruusbroec, invites all persons, whether good or bad, to union with divinity. If a person ignores the call, the individual gives up other gifts of God that would follow that union. God's grace makes it possible for every sinner to receive wisdom, forsake sin, and become a virtuous person, but that person must submit to God in all things.

LONGING FOR GOD

Some of God's gifts, however, can become an occasion for sin by the wicked, such gifts as health, beauty, wisdom, riches, and worldly honor. These are the least valuable of God's gifts. With these, he said, "the good serve God and his friends, while the wicked serve the world, the flesh, and the devil."[11]

The active life, for Ruusbroec, was a matter of keeping the commandments of God. Some people condemn the contemplative, thinking that those who practice contemplation are guilty of idleness. Martha made that complaint about Mary. However, others cannot possibly know what is going on in a person's interior life. They have no idea what it means to gaze upon God's resplendence. The true contemplative who has completely given himself up to God, dying in God, fulfills what was written in Colossians 3:3, "For you have died, and your life is hidden with Christ in God."

So, how do we do this? Ruusbroec has provided us with a roadmap. First, we take all our works and our very selves as an offering when we seek to enter into God's presence, after which we leave behind ourselves and all our works. As he put it, "Dying in love, we will transcend all our creatureliness, and attain to God's superessential richness. There we will possess God in an eternal dying to ourselves."[12] He added, "For our mind, our life, our very being are raised up in a state of oneness and united with the truth which is God himself."[13] This deep experience with God generates a hunger that is never satisfied. Immersion in God is characterized by habitual love. It generates virtue and makes us better people. Ruusbroec wrote, "We feel an eternal inclination toward something which is different from what we are ourselves."[14]

For Ruusbroec, our union with God is not an identification. We will always be different from God. Our experience of the resplendence of God teaches us truth about love and virtue.

In *The Sparkling Stone*, Ruusbroec listed four ways of experiencing our union with God. First, we experience God's grace:

God's love and forgiveness. "God," he wrote, "enlightens, gladdens, and makes fruitful everyone who wishes to obey him."[15] We must, however, help God by our own free will to enkindle the fire of his love within us. What is required are such things as interior fervor, going out of ourselves to others with fraternal love and fidelity, descending beneath ourselves by penance, and rising above ourselves through works of devotion.

Second, we experience ourselves as embraced by God. With a simple gaze beyond reason and a willing inclination, we sense God's embrace.

Third, when we experience transformation in God, we will feel ourselves "swallowed up in the groundless abyss of our eternal blessedness."[16]

Fourth, when we try to analyze or examine the experience, we fall back on reasoning and become aware of the distinction between God and ourselves. God is outside of ourselves "in all his incomprehensibility," and so we experience an "eager craving." This draws us out of ourselves and our souls open to "taste and see" God.[17]

Ruusbroec tried to develop a deeper inner life by serving a church in a city, but eventually, the noise, crowds, and other distractions were too much and, with two colleagues, he fled to the woods and developed a community of hermits. They would live together, yet keep to themselves as much as possible. John liked to go out into nature to write.

He did not believe that we all should become hermits. Whatever our state in life, we can cultivate a deep inner life, beginning with living a life of virtue. Ruusbroec reminds us that a meeting between a person and God occurs in love, by becoming lost in the mystery of God, a mystery that is free of images as we develop our inner lives. He wrote about a world many of us do not know, but he challenged us to seek it, a world of inner transformation that we can only vaguely imagine until we have experienced it.

LONGING FOR GOD

Dom Cuthbert Butler in *Western Mysticism* said of Ruusbroec, "It may with all probability be said that other than him there has been no greater contemplative; and certainly there has been no greater mystical writer. Whether in the sublimity of his elevations or in the power of recording his experiences, Ruusbroec stands as one of the very greatest of mystics."[18]

FURTHER READING

Ruusbroec, John. *The Spiritual Espousals and Other Works.* Translated by James A. Wiseman, OSB. The Classics of Western Spirituality. New York: Paulist Press, 1985.

8

THE QUAKER TRADITION

The Light of God Within

He was languishing in jail again. The place was disgusting, and he had nothing in common with his fellow inmates. They had committed crimes. He was there for preaching that there is something of God in every person. The established churches always resented dissent. They had the truth, and those who disagreed were a danger to society. Dissenters are hard to control, especially if they claim to have had experiences with God.

George Fox (1624–91) had wandered around the cities and towns of England seeking a satisfying religion. The Church of England was impressive. The architecture of the buildings invited meditation and faith. The liturgy was grand and colorful with a variety of priestly and episcopal vestments. The classical music touched his heart. But something was lacking.

He visited the Baptists in their plain and simple churches and liked their enthusiasm and commitment. Their love of the Bible, strict moralism, and energetic preaching were appealing, but something was lacking there, too. The Presbyterians were calmer people who wanted everything done decently and in order. That was not enough for him. What was he to do? He was only a leather worker and sometime shepherd, but he was intelligent enough.

As he continued his quest, George Fox began to have a series of mystical experiences in which he discovered Christ living in him. He sensed interior movements of the Holy Spirit. Religion, he began to believe, was a matter of the inner life. What he found lacking in the churches and movements he encountered was an awareness of the interior presence of God in every person. His sense that there is "that of God in every person" became a basic belief.

Eventually, he was freed from prison, though he would see the inside of five others. He began to attract a devoted group of followers, and some of them would also find themselves in prison. Many of them trembled or quaked when they stood before judges. Hence, the name Quakers came to be applied to them. In time their official name would be The Society of Friends, somewhat reminiscent of the fourteenth-century mystical movement, the Friends of God.

The Quakers' dominant belief is that there is an Inner Light in each of us, a divine element, which, if we are attentive to it, will reveal the reality of God to us. Worship is a matter of sitting in silence, listening for the Holy Spirit. On occasion it would move a person to stand up and speak about his or her faith. For Quakers there are no sacraments and no professional ministry. There is no official doctrine or creed. An effort to make such a statement resulted in a book, *Christian Faith and Practice*. However, instead of spelling out doctrines, the book became an anthology of Quakers' spiritual experiences.

Robert Barclay, a seventeenth-century Quaker intellectual, wrote about one of his experiences: "When I came into the silent assembly of God's people, I felt a secret power among them,

The Quaker Tradition

which touched my heart, and as I gave way to it, I found the evil in me weakening and the good raised up."[1]

One of the foundational assumptions of the Quakers is that revelation did not end with the closing of the New Testament canon—it is still taking place. Every person has the potential to experience the presence of God.

Two other important Quaker beliefs are pacifism and social service. Their best-known agency is the American Friends Service Committee, which provides social and humanitarian work and peace advocacy all over the world. It was awarded the Nobel Peace Prize in 1947. Quakers see themselves as neither Catholic nor Protestant, but as a third force, a part of the mystical stream that has nurtured the whole church throughout its history.

The lives of the three twentieth-century Quakers presented in this chapter were intertwined in several ways. All three studied philosophy at Harvard, although not at the same time, and they taught at Haverford College in Philadelphia, the leading Quaker college, where their teaching careers overlapped.

RUFUS JONES (1863–1948)

A college student was taking a walk in a French forest glade. Surrounded by the beauties of nature he was thinking about his life and what its meaning might be. The trees, the sounds of birds, the moving water in a creek, and the small animal life provided a pleasant context for serious pondering. The light filtered through the trees and the fragrant smell of the vegetation generated a sense of peace and stillness. He was trying to discover some central purpose for his future and wondered if he would ever find it. As he pondered this question, he had a formative experience that influenced him the rest of his life. He felt "the walls between the visible and invisible suddenly grow thin," and he became conscious of a "definite mission in life" opening out before him. It was a fleeting moment, too elusive to "catch and hold." He knelt down alone, and in the beauty and silence of the moment in the green forest, but with a sense of "an Invading Life," Rufus Jones dedicated himself to studying the depths of the human soul and how it was related to God.

Jones and a cousin were living temporarily in a small French village with a Protestant pastor, hoping to improve their use of the French language. In fact, they agreed to speak only French while they were there. This unexpected mystical experience in France changed his life forever.[2]

Jones was born in 1863 on a farm near South China, Maine, to devout Quaker parents. He led the normal life of a farm boy in those days, doing the chores, looking after animals, and working in the fields. He attended Quaker meetings with his parents and grew to appreciate the silence and the style of the Quaker tradition. He attended several Quaker schools and eventually Haverford College in Philadelphia, where he received a bachelor's and a master's degree. Later, he spent a year at Harvard and received a second master's, studying with some of the best-known philosophers in America. It was a thrilling experience for him that was intellectually stimulating and opened a new world of knowledge to him.

He taught philosophy at Haverford for forty years and became a man of enormous influence among Quakers. He published fifty-four books. Among them were *Studies in Mystical Religion, The Flowering of Mysticism, New Studies in Mystical Religion*—consisting of lectures given at Union Theological Seminary in New York—*Some Exponents of Mystical Religion*, and *Spiritual Reformers in the 16th and 17th Centuries*. He also edited and helped write a six-volume history of the Society of Friends as well as the classic *The Faith and Practice of the Quakers*.

Jones traveled extensively during his career, meeting Quakers in England and throughout Europe. He was honorary chairman of the American Friends Service Committee when it received the Noble Peace Prize and soon became its first employed leader. He had many experiences and met a wide variety of people.

Jones was much loved by Quakers everywhere. An Englishman reflecting on the influence that Jones had on him wrote, "To a whole generation of us he was a prophet and a saint and a shining light. We loved him and we venerated him. He was the leader of our lives. His writing was secondary. It was his personality, his outgoing love, his humor, his geniality, his luminousness. The Holy Spirit was in him to his fingertips. He made each of us feel worthwhile."[3]

How did Jones understand mysticism? In *Studies in Mystical Religion*, he defined it as "the type of religion which puts the emphasis on immediate awareness of a relation with God, on direct and intimate consciousness of the Divine Presence. It is religion at its most acute, intense, and living stage."[4] Mysticism, he knew, is not confined just to Christianity; it is seen in many other religions.

Jones was convinced that experiences of a Higher Presence are as old as the human personality. In *A Call to What Is Vital*, he wrote that the consciousness of a direct relation with God is not confined to a particular class of people. It is found in the "democratic laity" as well as the "high pulpit class." An awareness of transcendence is "a trait of our being."[5] The Society of Friends assumed that all members receive the Divine Light, which enables them to express more than just ordinary wisdom. People can experience the "invading power of God in everyday life."

What happens to a person who has had a mystical encounter with God? Jones wrote about "an enlarged area of life." One's horizons are widened and the person connects with "the beyond." The individual becomes more dynamic in his or her life. There is more unity of personality, and an increase in creative energy.

Jones made use of three academic disciplines in his efforts to study mysticism: psychology, which studies our mental processes; philosophy, with its emphasis on critical thinking; and history, which teaches us about human experience. As a professor of philosophy at Haverford, he devoted his life to a study of mysticism and wanted to use all the tools of responsible academic scholarship in his pursuit of knowledge.

The first chapter in Jones's *Studies in Mystical Religion* is on "The Mystical Element in Primitive Christianity," which he defined as the first few years in the life of the Church. As described in the Book of Acts, early Christians were a mystical fellowship. Jones saw Christians as bound together, not by an external organization, but by the experience of the Divine Presence among the members. Jones noted that the duration of that kind of church was very short because it soon became organized and a structure of authority developed. The institution became dominant over experience. Jones believed that at its heart Christianity is a mystical religion, and at its best, Christians experience what Christ experienced—the presence of God developing in us a new creation.[6]

For Jones, Paul was an example of the primitive spirit. His gospel was grounded in an immediate encounter with the Divine on the road to Damascus. Jones said, "It impinged upon him, invaded him, and became the inward principle of his very self." He cited passages such as Galatians 2:20, "It is no longer I who live, but it is Christ who lives in me," and Romans 8:11, "If the Spirit of him who raised Jesus from the dead dwells in you, he who raised Christ from the dead will give life to your mortal bodies." And, of course, he mentioned Paul's own mystical experience in 2 Corinthians 12.[7] For Jones, the abiding reality of God cannot be dogmatically asserted; it becomes real to us only in personal experience.[8]

Jones lived through the Great Depression of the 1930s. He said that if we don't rebuild our inner lives, we will only partly succeed in rebuilding the economic world. The deepest issues of life concern the soul, and as far as he could see, the Depression was caused by a condition of the soul: human greed. He was certain we would continue to suffer economic disasters from time to time because greed dominates economic life. Many problems in the world are at their root spiritual issues.

One of the issues that interested Jones was the relationship between science and religion. In his final book, written in 1948, Jones had an essay on "The Place of Prayer in a Scientific Age." With reference to evolution and creationism he wrote, "Faith is not endangered by the advance of science. It is endangered by the stagnation of religious conceptions."[9]

True prayer, Jones believed, "is immediate spiritual fellowship. It is an end in itself. It is the reason for being. The human heart is as sensitive to God as the retina is to light."[10] Prayer is a matter of being open to a Divine Presence and reaching out to the One who reaches out to us. Knowing God in human life is always a possibility, a possibility that transforms and enriches those who are open to it. The ultimate purpose of prayer is to build a relationship with God that enables an awareness of the Divine Presence.

Rufus Jones devoted his life to the study of religious experience and how we may encounter the presence of God in our lives. He has left us the results of very deep study. That a man would devote his life to this work is a remarkable gift to all religious people. Studying the work of Jones stimulates an awareness of the possibilities of mystical growth.

THOMAS KELLY (1893–1941)

A man had worked for years on a PhD dissertation at Harvard. Day after day, when he had completed his teaching duties, he would go to his study at home, close the door, and work until late in the evening. The room was cluttered with books and journals, marked-up pages that needed revision, and unorganized notes that might be difficult to find later. He was always researching, writing, rewriting, seeking a determined but elusive perfection. He already had that same degree from a smaller, less prestigious institution, but he believed a Harvard doctorate would open the doors to academic and scholarly success. Harvard saw no need for him to pursue a PhD, since he already had one, but his vigorous protests had been successful in changing the faculty's mind. He had published his dissertation and it received a good review in a philosophical journal. Now he had to overcome the final barrier, the oral defense of his work.

Nervous and beginning to perspire, he sat before a panel of the most distinguished philosophers in America, ready to answer their questions and demonstrate his brilliance.

The questioning began, but his mind went blank. In spite of all the study and research he had done, he could not think of anything to say. The faculty rephrased the questions, hoping to stimulate a response, but to no avail. In spite of all his study and determination, his mind failed him. What could he possibly do to redeem the situation? Nothing the professors said could stimulate his memory. What would they think of him, these philosophers that he had so long admired and studied? He could see their frowns and doubting demeanors.

This had happened before, but he had always recovered. Now questions about the work to which he had so singularly devoted himself, even to the point of neglecting his wife and children, seemed meaningless. How could he have forgotten so much? Years of study and research had produced no intelligent responses to the faculty he had respected and revered. His silence confounded them, but there was nothing to do but to tell him that he would never have a PhD from Harvard.

It was a crushing disappointment, and he returned to Haverford depressed and, in his own mind, disgraced. It was a terrible homecoming. How could he show his face on the campus? What would his students think? Would he lose his job? Would his family, which had sacrificed so much, be disappointed with him?

The Quaker Tradition

This unfortunate graduate student, Thomas Kelly, was born into a Quaker family on June 4, 1893. His childhood was not easy. His father died when he was only four years old, leaving himself, his sister, his mother, and a grandmother to fend for themselves on the family farm. In 1903, his mother moved the family to Wilmington, Ohio, where she took a business course for a year and found a job with the Irwin Auger Bit Company.

Kelly attended public schools and then enrolled in Wilmington College, a Quaker school from which he graduated. He had a love for science and majored in chemistry. While a student, he began to develop within himself a determination for perfection. He had serious religious interests and wanted to be a perfect Quaker. This carried over into his intellectual and academic life. He made high grades, which came from rigorous self-discipline and hard work.

Upon graduation, he received a scholarship to attend Haverford College for a year and receive a second bachelor's degree. He loved the East Coast academic atmosphere. It was intellectually stimulating, professors were admired, and there was constant discussion of important issues in the various fields of study. One of the most important influences on him was Rufus Jones, who introduced Kelly to the field of philosophy. Perhaps Jones could help him relate his interest as a science major in college to his love of the Quaker tradition. The two had somehow seemed unrelated. Was there a connection between his love for the laboratory and his search for the Inner Light?

Rufus Jones was concerned that contemporary Quakerism had strayed from its roots. He wanted it to return to the kind of mystical religion it had originally been. In Jones, Kelly found a kindred spirit who would be a lifelong friend, and he began working on a master's degree in philosophy. The Midwestern Quakerism in which Kelly had grown up was evangelical in style, more like a conservative Protestant church. Jones's mystical approach was something new to him.

LONGING FOR GOD

After Haverford, Kelly taught at a school in Canada for two years, where a group of Quakers encouraged him to go to Japan as a missionary. First, however, he would have to attend seminary. He entered Hartford Theological Seminary in the fall of 1916, excited about the stimulation the seminary would offer. He studied Hebrew and the New Testament with the same energy he had once studied chemistry. After a visit with Rufus Jones, Kelly abandoned the Japan mission and began to prepare for pastoral ministry. There had been some inner conflict between a desire for the Japan mission and his love for American Quakerism. The Quakers won in his mind. When the United States declared war on Germany in 1917, Kelly, as a pacifist, applied to work in a British YMCA canteen and counsel with the troops. He said that he hoped to bring "something of the spirit of Christ to other people."[11]

He eventually transferred to work with German POWs in England. He wrote home, "This prison work is more nearly what Christ would have done, as I understand his life and motives."[12] Eventually, he worked in the London office and made weekly inspections of the prison camps. In December 1917, Kelly and his YMCA associates were relieved of their duties and sent home. Having antiwar pacifists around was regarded as dangerous by the military. It might demoralize the troops as they thought about killing enemy soldiers whom they did not even know.

While in England, Kelly realized that what he really wanted to do was to teach in a college. He soon received an offer from Wilmington College, but he decided to finish seminary first. In 1919, he married Lael Macy, a minister's daughter, taught at Wilmington for two years, then returned to Hartford to work on a PhD. When the time came to defend his dissertation, his mind went blank, the nightmare of all graduate students. However, he was given a second chance and performed well.

Upon graduation he had two job offers. One was to teach philosophy at Earlham College in Indiana. The other was to go to Germany with the American Friends Service Committee (AFSC).

The Quaker Tradition

He accepted the Earlham appointment, but it was delayed a year so he could do foreign service. The AFSC wanted Kelly and his wife to nurture an infant Quaker movement in Germany. They discovered that many Germans were attracted to pacifism after the horrors of World War I. A permanent Quaker center was established in Berlin. After fifteen months, the Kellys returned to Indiana and Thomas began his teaching career at Earlham. His first two years were very happy. He began to preach frequently at Quaker meetings. In one of his sermons he said, "Down in the depths of our being there are inner fountains of divine life, ready to well up and flow forth." A central point, he said, is "that the human is in contact with the divine, nay that the very spring and fountain of our inner life and consciousness is the Eternal Spirit."[13] In expressing this fundamental Quaker belief, the mystical side of Kelly was beginning to emerge.

Kelly emphasized that the presence of God can be known in the ordinary, mundane, normal routines of daily life. He said there are times when we have "dreamy, mystical" thoughts and a sense of elevation when our thinking soars to great heights. But he was interested in the ordinary, often monotonous routines of life, as a context for mystical encounters. He said he did not want a God who lived on a mountain. He wanted a God on our level, a God who can see men working in fields and stores and women who toil and carry the household cares. He wanted a God who saw the "little frictions and annoyances that make life difficult."

His experiences at Earlham began to sour. During his trip to Germany, he became appreciative of Quaker mysticism but did not find it among the Friends in the Midwest. The idea of the Inner Light was not a central thought in many Quakers. The focus was on service, which he called "a splendid thing," but saw that it did not grow out of an experience of the presence of God. Indiana Quakers did not respond to his spirituality.

In the fall of 1930, he took a year's leave of absence to study at Harvard. He believed that the faculty there had the

LONGING FOR GOD

most influential group of philosophers in the Western world. He studied under the direction of Alfred North Whitehead, a British mathematician, who took his starting point in philosophy from the sciences—appropriate for Kelly, a science major.

After his studies at Harvard, Kelly had no desire to return to Earlham and the Midwest. During the Depression years there were no other college teaching opportunities. Unhappily, he returned to Earlham. He was determined, however, to prove himself as a competent scholar and philosopher. He worked long hours to perfect everything he did. The next five years were an unhappy time for Kelly. He found fault in everything at Earlham and felt there was no place for him in the Quaker community. He would come home from class and retire to his study, working on his doctoral dissertation, neglecting his wife and children. During these years, his intellectual life reached its peak, and he still clung to his basic Quaker idea that God could be known through mystical experience.

In December 1934, he suffered a nervous breakdown. His years of hard work without any rest and his personal disappointment that he had to return to Earlham took their toll. He made it to class, but teaching wore him out. He had to take naps between classes and spent the weekends in bed. His wife had to drive him to the campus.

Against the advice of Rufus Jones, he accepted a position at the University of Hawaii. It was only a one-year appointment. Beyond the larger salary, he saw this as an opportunity to get closer to the East and to study Eastern religion and philosophy. He wanted to broaden his knowledge of the world and other philosophies. He hoped to defend his dissertation at Harvard before he left for Hawaii, but the faculty advised that he should wait until his return.

While in Hawaii, he received an offer from Haverford College. He saw it as the opportunity of a lifetime, the fulfillment of his dreams and a chance to reconnect with the Quakers. He

The Quaker Tradition

developed friendships with Rufus Jones and Douglas Steere, the chairman of the philosophy department. Both men shared Kelly's interest in the mystical tradition. Now was the time for his dissertation examination. As we have already seen, that experience was a disaster.

It was a stunning blow. His son wrote, "It was as if the world had caved in on him."[14] His wife feared that he might have a fatal breakdown or commit suicide or sink into a depression from which he would never recover. Douglas Steere and the president of Haverford assured him that this would have no effect on his standing at Haverford, and the failure would not be made public.

In late 1937, Kelly described "being shaken by the experience of Presence, something that I did not seek, but that sought me."[15] Perhaps the failure at Harvard had made him more receptive to God.

The change in Kelly became obvious when he spoke to a Young Friend's group in January 1938. His style was different. As his son put it, "He was no longer the erudite college professor describing an experience he had read [about] or observed in others, but was sharing the very intimacy of his own life with them."[16] Thereafter, he wrote and spoke out of his own experience of the Divine Presence.

In the summer of 1938, Kelly went back to Germany on a trip that Rufus Jones and others had worked out for him. American Quakers were concerned about the welfare of Quakers living under Adolf Hitler. Kelly was welcomed by many German Quakers who remembered his earlier visit. He was expected to assess the situation and offer the love and concern of those in the United States.

At one point in his visit, he crossed the border into France so he could write home without fear of German censorship. He told his wife that he could not use names and places in his letters. He wrote, "Until you have lived in this world of despair and fear and abysmal suffering of the soul, you can never know how serious the consequences of a chance anecdote may be in the way of imprisonment, beatings with clubs, family separations, and death. This is the first lesson you must learn in Germany."[17]

The German experience caused him to question his own lifestyle in America. Living in comfortable circumstances at Haverford in parklike surroundings with such privileges while the world was aflame caused him to wonder what he could offer a suffering world. After seeing the suffering of people in Germany under Nazism, he realized the consequences of an absence of love. He had a sense God was helping him to see that God's final nature is love, and not to realize this caused the inhumanity he witnessed.

When Kelly returned to America in September 1938, he was the last person off the ship. He seemed to be in a daze. His brother-in-law, Robert Whitehead, said that after talking with him that evening, he felt that compared to Kelly, he had no religion at all. The return to parklike surroundings was difficult. He experienced dryness in his spiritual life, for the intense experiences he had earlier with God were brief, passing moments. He knew he had to make changes in his life.

Kelly renewed his relationship with his family and began to show more love. He would come home from teaching and play with his children. The family had a small cabin on the coast of Maine where they enjoyed the summers. He invited students into his home to read spiritual classics together and discuss them. The time at Haverford was generally a happy time for Kelly. A book editor called and asked if Kelly had a manuscript his company could publish. He began work on what would be published after his death, *A Testament of Devotion*.[18]

The first article in Kelly's book explains his understanding of "The Light Within." Deep within each of us, he wrote, is a Divine Center to which we may continuously return. Here, he said "is the 'Slumbering Christ,' stirring to be awakened. And he is within us all."[19] But how do we access the Inner Light?

The Quaker Tradition

The answer for Kelly was establishing habits of "inward orientation," warning that it is a slow process. He wrote, "An inner, secret turning to God can be made steady, after weeks and months and years of practice and lapses and failures and returns." He advised his readers, "Walk and talk and work and laugh with your friends. But behind the scenes, keep up the life of simple prayer and inward worship. The first days and weeks and months are awkward and painful, but enormously rewarding."[20] But longer discipline in this inward prayer will establish more enduring upward-reaching prayer and submission and relaxed listening in the depths.[21]

On a January morning in 1941, Kelly said to his wife, "Today will be the greatest day of my life." That evening, while drying the dishes after supper, he suddenly died from a massive heart attack at only forty-nine years of age.

On the weekend before his death, he had written a little piece for the 1941 meeting of the Friends World Committee. It was about the Inner Light that is present in every person. He said that the Inner Light is shining in souls. It is present in small Quaker groups. It will help bear up those who work in the world of need. It is a wonder that it is at work within us.

Kelly's life was a life of accomplishments and disappointments. The accomplishments filled him with knowledge. The disappointments turned him around and gave him new life. "All things work together for good for those who love God, who are called according to his purpose" (Rom 8:28).

DOUGLAS STEERE (1901–1995)

Life in the Maria Laach monastery, founded in Germany in 1093, was a wonderful experience for him. It was located by a beautiful lake surrounded by tall trees and lush vegetation, a fine setting for a contemplative monastery. There was a sense of beauty and an atmosphere of peace. The German Romanesque buildings with their many towers and a church with an apse at each end were impressive. Attending the daily round of the Divine Offices, as the services were called, and hearing the monks chant the psalms throughout the day had a rich, deepening effect on him.

He was there for an academic sabbatical. The quiet atmosphere, the contemplative spirit, and the richly stocked library provided opportunities for the study of spirituality. He read the Rule of St. Benedict, one of the founders of Western monasticism, as well as the works of the mystics: Bernard of Clairvaux, Hildegard of Bingen, and Teresa of Avila. Later, he would become interested in Dorothy Day and Thomas Merton. All were Catholics. These people had so much wisdom, and the monastic life provided a fruitful context for prayer and spiritual growth he found hard to resist. As he walked the halls of the monastery, prayed in the church, meditated in the cloister garden, and chatted with the monks, he could not help but realize that Roman Catholicism was rich in spiritual resources. Liturgy, devotional practices, and discipline were very attractive to him. It was time for him to make a decision about identifying with a religious tradition to order and guide his life. Catholicism, especially in a monastic setting, was very impressive. Is that the way he should go? Would that Church help him develop a rich spiritual life?

However, he was a professor at a Quaker college. The Quakers' silent worship, their commitments to pacifism and social justice, and their mystical heritage were also attractive. His Quaker colleagues were exceptional people, and he did not take their deep faith lightly. What was Douglas Steere to do? How should he decide? Catholic or Quaker? Whichever route he chose would impact the rest of his life. Like many before him, Steere found the faith of Rufus Jones impossible to resist. After wrestling with the agony of uncertainty, he became a convinced Quaker in 1933.

Douglas Steere went on to become one of the leading Quakers of the mid-twentieth century. His influence was enormous, his contacts with others were wide, and his thought was ever

The Quaker Tradition

open to new ideas and experiences. He was much in demand as the Quaker Observer delegate to the Second Vatican Council in the 1960s and was active in the ecumenical movement, serving with both the National and World Councils of Churches. He traveled the world for the American Friends Service Committee.

His religious interests were broad. He often quoted Jewish writers. He organized dialogues between Christians and Buddhists in Japan and Christians and Hindus in India. He said that life was "lent to be spent." He was also interested in those who transcended religious barriers. He cared deeply about people and was known for affirming and encouraging others. Glenn Hinson, a Southern Baptist church historian, said, "I never met with him that I did not go away buoyed up and filled with some of his contagious and well-founded optimism."[22] Steere was an example of a Christian who combined both the active and contemplative lives.

In July 1945, at the end of World War II in Europe, he led the organizing of a Quaker relief effort in Finland, a country that had suffered greatly during the war. For this work, the Finnish government awarded him the Declaration of Knight First Class of the White Rose in Finland in 1987. At an early meeting of Quakers to plan the relief effort, he reported in a letter to his wife, Dorothy:

"About 8:50, I gave a brief prayer that came of itself and then Fred Tritten prayed, and in a flash, I was melted down and the glorious release of the life of God was mine in an instant. My face was wet with tears and I felt that nothing in the world mattered that could disturb this certainty, and I felt ever so close to each one there, and as we closed, I saw two others who seemed to be having the same experience."[23]

Who was this mystic? Steere was born in 1901, in Harbor Beach, Michigan, where his father worked for a railroad. He graduated from high school at age sixteen, having skipped a grade in elementary school.

LONGING FOR GOD

While a student at Michigan Agricultural College, which later became Michigan State University, he began a serious religious search. One of his professors urged him to go to Harvard and study philosophy. The impact of that experience was surprising. Steere said that the first year at Harvard wiped out what little faith he had. A cauldron of new ideas left little room for belief in God. He said, "I touched bottom and saw little to live for."[24]

Fortunately, he met a Chinese student who told Steere of his conversion from communism to Christianity. He met some students from the Episcopal Divinity School near Harvard who gathered for silent prayer at noon. He never became a regular in that group, but it did open him to the reality of prayer. By the end of his first year at Harvard, his faith had been renewed, which he attributed to the practice of silent prayer. Later, he would see the contemplative life as "a continual discovery of Christ in new and unexpected places."[25]

His philosophy studies began to flourish. He was invited to join Phi Beta Kappa. After two years he qualified for the PhD program, but before he could begin that work, he received a Rhodes Scholarship to study at Oxford, where he would receive a bachelor's and a master's degree. It was there that he discovered the Quakers. He said that it was among them that he discovered the power of Christ's indwelling spirit within himself.

He loved the silence of a Quaker meeting where no one spoke unless moved by the Holy Spirit, although he observed that not everyone followed the Quaker motto, "When in doubt, wait." He wrote affectionately about such occasions: "There is a melting down, a tendering in which each feels closely knit to the common Father and his fellows. I have seen this silent worship level a group in which there was an ugly barrier separating two of its members and I have seen it begin them to ask forgiveness."[26]

Having completed his two degrees at Oxford, he returned to the United States. In 1931, he received a PhD from Harvard with a dissertation on Baron Friedrich von Hügel, a liberal Roman

The Quaker Tradition

Catholic British philosopher and theologian and author of *The Mystical Element of Religion*. Steere had already come to the attention of Rufus Jones, who invited him to join the faculty at Haverford in 1928. He would later be Jones's successor as chair of the philosophy department.

Steere would gain wide recognition as a scholar, theologian, and philosopher. He was a member of the American Theological Society (where he played a leading role), the American Philosophical Association, and a group of younger theologians called the Young Christian Thinkers. He and Jones were active in founding Pendle Hill, an important resource of Quaker life and a retreat center.

Steere's spirituality was grounded in a belief in God's initiative. It is God who seeks us. "The core of the Christian religion," he wrote, "is to be found in this personal solicitation by God…a caring that gives to each individual his worth."[27] If God is seeking us, Steere also believed that we are seeking God.

There is a yearning for the living God, there is "a watermark hidden away deep within the soul of every [person] that no collective or personal distortion can ever fully blot out, and it is this in which these men and women respond to the intensely active siege of every soul by God, a siege that never ceases."[28]

For Quakers, this infinite worth of every person was because of the Inner Light, that spark of the Divine that is in every person. George Fox had said, "In every [person], there is something that is not of dust or earth or flesh or time, but of God."[29] For Steere, being a Christian is not a matter of what we do but who we are.

His book *On Beginning from Within* is about saints—what makes a person a saint and how saints influence us. We have all known saintly people, people who have some unique quality about them that both impresses and moves us. We want to be around them and we wish we could be like them. They embody the deepest longings within us. Saints are not naïve about human nature, because they know what sin is—they have known it in themselves—but they are not overcome by it because they also know the Inner Light.

One of the more interesting parts of *On Beginning from Within* is on the relationship between devotion and theology. Steere wrote, "Great theology comes from great devotion."[30] Theology, he believed, must be more than an intellectual exercise. For mystics, the deepest theology comes out of their experience of God.

In addition to its emphasis on the mystical life, the Quaker church is also known as a peace church. There is a strong tradition of conscientious objection to military service, and many young Quakers have suffered as a result. Steere worked for peace at the international level. During his 1933–34 sabbatical, he established many important relationships in Europe. In an effort to encourage German Quakers, he made a risky visit to Germany in 1937 while Hitler was in power and the threat of war was real, and again in 1940, after the war in Europe had begun. He was active in the Fellowship of Reconciliation, one of the leading peace organizations in the world, and served as chair of the American section from 1954 to 1966.

Steere was also strongly committed to the ecumenical movement. He was interested, however, in spiritual, not denominational, unions. In his book *Together in Solitude*, he identified three areas of common concern among Catholics and Protestants. The first was spiritual direction. He wrote, "It would seem that Catholics and non-Catholics alike must admit the need of adequate personal counsel for those who feel a yearning to put their lives more completely in God's hands."[31] He raised an interesting question: "How do I become a Christian when I already am one? We are all unfinished creatures." Spiritual direction, as Steere understood it, was "guiding people to make progress in the practice of communion with God."[32]

His second area of common interest was private prayer. He said, "Prayer is daring to read the text of the universe in the original."[33] To know God directly is to find out who we are. Beyond

The Quaker Tradition

our individual experience, the search for God binds us with others who have the same concern. Catholics and Protestants may never have institutional unity, but there is a more important unity among seekers of God.

The third concern was our sense of responsibility to the human family. Many have commitments to peace, civil rights, and justice for all people, and these unite us. Steere said that the traditions of Catholic charity and Protestant service are reconfirmed in every generation of Christians who see that Christ's body is truly found in those who need help.

Steere is also known for his interest in the mystical tradition. In *Together in Solitude*, he defined *mysticism* as "direct and immediate touch with ultimate reality."[34] He examined many of the questions raised about mystical experience.

Can mystical experience be communicated? The problem is that we do not have the language capable of communicating such mystery. How does one explain the unexplainable? For most of the people studied in this book there is no sensory experience to describe. There is no adequate psychological category to identify it. Some have said that the only way to know what it is, is to experience it yourself. In Paul's experience described in 2 Corinthians 12, he said he heard things that cannot be told. We do not have the ability to describe an indescribable experience.

A related issue is the role of tradition in mystical experience. Christian, Hindu, Buddhist, Muslim, and Jewish mystics receive such experiences in their own religious context. Steere wondered why the experiences of some negate the value of the created world, while others seem to embrace it. Why do some write of the complete loss of personality, while others find personality affirmed and enhanced? Why do some mystics turn inward and ignore the world, while the experience of others leads them into service to the human family?

Then there is the question of whether mystical experience can be acquired, or is it a gift of God over which we have no control?

LONGING FOR GOD

Can one prepare oneself for such an experience, or is there nothing anyone can do to induce it?

Steere expressed his own understanding of mysticism as "the ravishing, energizing, quickening power of the order that impinges upon our own and that the mystical breakthrough gives such inexpressible delight and refreshment to the soul."[35] He referred to a comment of Bernard of Clairvaux that a mystical encounter with God is a brief and fleeting experience, just enough to have an impact on us, but not enough for us to probe and analyze it. It comes and goes but has a profound effect.

To the question of whether mysticism is a gift or is acquired, Steere said that "the weight is on the side of being utterly given."[36] He noted, however, that it requires a willingness to be transformed by it. That is a controversial conclusion, but Steere suggested that many would like an experience with God, but do not want to change their lives.

One of Steere's most popular books was *Dimensions of Prayer*, first published in 1962 and revised by his wife in 1997. In this book, Steere said, "Prayer is for the religious life what original research is for science."[37] It is a response to God's initiative in seeking us. It is the most open way to come near to God. It has a transforming power on us and often leads us into the unknown. The sign of true prayer is charity; it pushes us to action, to "an ethical sharpening that is dangerous to complacency." In prayer, he wrote "we are brought inwardly before a revolutionary leveling of God's infinite concern for every soul that comes into the world."[38]

Douglas Steere lived that concept. He was a man of deep prayer, with mystical tendencies, who traveled the world working for peace and human good. He and Dorothy were known for their incredible energy. No trip was too arduous, no duty was impossible. They gave themselves with unbelievable generosity. It is sad that during the last five years of his life he suffered from Alzheimer's disease. A great mind was stilled, but all who believe

The Quaker Tradition

in the importance of prayer, contemplation, and concern for the human family will find great value in his rich and productive life. He died in 1996.

Quaker spirituality begins and ends with a belief that there is something of God in every person, and this is the foundation of our spiritual quest. Worship is then a matter of listening for the Holy Spirit.

Although the three men studied in this book had mystical inclinations, they were active in the world, even to the extent of the American Friends Service Committee winning the Nobel Peace Prize. They were pacifists, concerned with all aspects of human life. One traveled to Germany during the Hitler regime. Another helped in the restoration of Finland after the war. There are many other examples of the Quaker connection with social action and the mystical quest. If we are committed to social justice, we can still develop a deep inner life. If we are mystically inclined, there is still work in the world for us to do.

FURTHER READING

Steere, Douglas V., ed. *Quaker Spirituality: Selected Writings*. The Classics of Western Spirituality. New York: Paulist Press, 1984.

9

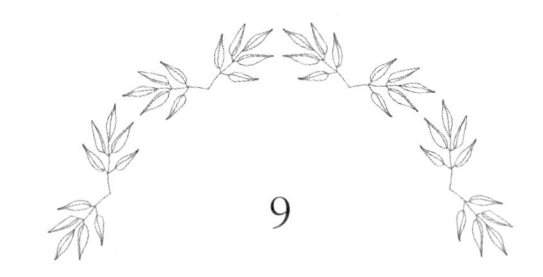

HOWARD THURMAN

1899–1981
Creative Ministry

Howard Thurman, now fourteen years old, arrived at the Daytona train station, bound for Jacksonville. A cousin in another town had offered him room and board if he wanted to attend high school. The young man's hometown did not have a high school for African Americans. Their school only went through the seventh grade. The cousin's offer was a godsend that could open a whole new world. Young Howard dragged a battered trunk with a rope wrapped around it to the station, intending to check it on the train. The clerk refused to check it, however, because regulations required that the tag be attached to a handle, and that trunk had no handle. It would have to be sent express, but Thurman had no way to pay the express fee.

He sat down on the dirty brick station steps and cried his heart out. His opportunity for further education and a better future had vanished. After a few minutes, he looked up and saw a tall man in overalls and a denim cap who asked him why he was crying. He told the man he wanted a high school education in another town but did not have the money to ship this trunk by express. The man said, "If you're trying to get out of this damn town to get an education, the least I can do is help you." He walked over to the agent, opened a rawhide money bag, counted out the express fee, then disappeared without a word.[1] The world began to open. Years later, when he had become one of the most significant religious leaders of his time, Thurman would tell people how his life was radically changed by a stranger at a train station.

This African American boy in Florida was trying to make his way in a rigidly segregated society. Daytona, Florida, in the early twentieth century, was geographically divided between white and black, and crossing the line was a very rare occurrence. Thurman's grandmother, who inspired his faith, was a former slave. She could not read, so the young boy read the Bible to her. Although she loved hearing the stories told in the language of King James, she refused to listen to anything written by St. Paul because he had told slaves to obey their masters.

Was Thurman a mystic? Martin Marty, regarded by many as the dean of Protestant church historians, said that saints are difficult to find, but Howard Thurman would qualify. He was not a Quaker like Rufus Jones or Douglas Steere. Marty said that Thurman drew on the Quaker tradition by stumbling on it. At other times, he seemed predestined to be found by it.[2]

Luther E. Smith Jr., in his anthology of Thurman's writings, said, "Thurman is a mystic. He describes mysticism as a form of religious experience, where the awareness of a 'conscious and direct exposure,' to God is more intense. His mystic consciousness informed all his insights."[3]

After completing high school, and due to the generosity of another stranger, Thurman enrolled in Morehouse College in Atlanta, one of the premier African American colleges for men, majoring in economics. Morehouse was known for instilling a strong sense of self-worth and self-respect in students. Howard

Thurman drank deeply of that spirit and graduated at the top of his class.

He gradually developed an interest in ministry pursuits. During his time at Morehouse, he spent two summers in New York, studying at Columbia University. He did so well in the first course he took that it inflated his ego and he was, as he later described himself, a nuisance. Finally, one of his favorite professors at Morehouse told him not to speak any more in his class. That seemed to cure the problem. During his second summer at Columbia, he took a course on reflective thinking. Here he learned how to use reflective thinking in solving problems. He regarded it as "the most significant single course he ever took."[4] On Sundays he attended Fifth Avenue Presbyterian Church. He had never been in a church like this and was deeply impressed with its beauty and formalism. The summer minister was Dr. Hugo Black, who made a strong impression on Thurman by his manner and mind, and his skill as a preacher. Because of these experiences and the influence of some of his professors at Morehouse, he decided on ministry as his vocation by the beginning of his senior year.

The first seminary to which he applied had a policy of not admitting African Americans, but his next option, Rochester Theological Seminary, admitted two African Americans each year. The school was well-known as the heart of the Social Gospel in the United States. This was a movement that focused on poor people, labor, slums, and a variety of justice issues. Walter Rauschenbusch, a major leader in the movement, had been a Rochester professor, and that spirit was still alive in the school. It was the right place for Howard Thurman.

For the first time in his life, Thurman found himself immersed in the white community. This was a new experience, and he was not sure how to handle it. He made his way, however, and eventually graduated with the highest honors. As a student, he was invited by two white classmates to room with them. He accepted the invitation, although it violated a seminary policy that, fortunately, no one tried to enforce. These three students became lifetime friends, and Thurman learned how to be comfortable around white people.

There were several professors who particularly influenced him. Dr. Henry Burke Robbins "communicated the awe, the mystery, and the glory of the Presence." His course on the history of religion opened a new world to Thurman. Another, Dr. George Cross, taught systematic theology. Thurman said his lectures were carefully constructed and concise, but not without humor. The students often met with the professor on Saturdays to discuss questions they had from the lectures, which, he said, the professor often reduced to ash. Thurman wrote a seventy-page, carefully documented paper on Augustine that Cross rejected, saying the paper would be good for an average student but he was not average. He told him to rewrite a paper that would be worthy of him. He encouraged Thurman to explore new ideas.[5]

At Morehouse, he had been involved with the "Colored Branch" of the YMCA. In Rochester, the YMCA did not have such a branch, but the YWCA did, and Thurman was invited to teach in the adult education evening school. He began to receive invitations to speak at church services in many congregations that had never had any experience with a black man, and they often asked him to talk about the race issue. What was it like in the South? Had he been mistreated? How did black people keep up their courage and self-respect under such segregation? In several of these places, he had encounters with the Ku Klux Klan. With few African Americans in the area, targets of the Klan were usually Jews and Catholics, but Thurman had a few frightening confrontations.

During the summers, Thurman worked at a Baptist church in Roanoke, Virginia, gaining experience in the ministry. Eventually, he was ordained by that congregation. A week after graduation, he married Kate Kelly and became the pastor of Mount Zion

LONGING FOR GOD

Baptist Church in Oberlin, Ohio. It was there that he began to develop his preaching style, and the little church started to grow. While attending a conference on religious education, he bought a book, *Finding the Trail of Life in College*, by the Quaker Rufus Jones. He sat on the steps of the church where the conference was being held and read the book straight through without stopping. Thurman decided that he had to study with Jones.

A friend made an inquiry, and Jones sent a letter inviting Thurman to come to Haverford College for a semester and do an independent study with him. Thurman resigned from his church. His wife, who had been advised by her doctor to seek a warmer climate, returned to her family in Atlanta to convalesce from an illness, taking their daughter with her.

Arriving at Haverford in January 1929, he said, "I wanted so desperately to nourish the inner regions of my spirit, which even then were clamoring for attention." He received a grant from the National Council for Religion in Higher Education and moved into the graduate student dormitory for a semester.

Thurman attended all the lectures of Rufus Jones and participated in a seminar on the mystic Meister Eckhart, which he described as "exciting and stimulating beyond anything I had known before."[6] On Wednesday nights he often dropped in on Quaker meetings at which he was frequently asked to speak. Jones gave him reading assignments on mystical religion and the two of them had regular discussions. Thurman wrote several papers on well-known mystics.

At the end of the semester, he wrote an evaluation of his experience. "My study at Haverford was a crucial experience, a watershed from which flowed much of the thought and endeavor to which I was to commit the rest of my working life."[7] The importance of having a deep awareness of God's presence would reveal itself in many aspects of his ministry.

When his semester at Haverford was over, Thurman moved back to Atlanta where he received a dual appointment at both

Spelman College, a school for African American women, where he would teach Scripture, and at Morehouse, where he would teach religion and philosophy. His work in the New Testament at Spelman, he said, enabled him to explore more deeply the mind of Jesus. The women also needed a sense of their own worth. The oppressive racial climate of Atlanta and the South affected all of them, and the analogies resonated between their own situations and Jesus's life as a part of the Jewish minority in the Roman Empire.

During his second year in Atlanta, Thurman's wife died. His mother moved in with him to take care of his daughter, while he found himself emotionally and physically exhausted. He said that he needed to get his bearings on his future personally and professionally. A trip to Europe might help, the first of a number of trips overseas. After time in London and Scotland, he traveled to Paris and Geneva, returning home refreshed and renewed, ready for whatever life brought next.

In time, Thurman renewed a friendship with a woman he had known earlier, Sue Bailey, a traveling secretary for the national board of the YWCA. They had a long and happy marriage.

What came next was an offer to join the faculty of the School of Religion at Howard University in Washington, D.C., considered by many to be the leading university for African American students. Later, he would be appointed dean of the Chapel. Getting students to attend chapel with enthusiasm and without resentment was a huge challenge. Thurman experimented with different forms of worship in the hope of gaining their interest and improving their experience. Drawing on his study of the mystics at Haverford, he provided periods of silence for meditation and prayer. He also introduced liturgical dance. The first dancer was a Roman Catholic woman who taught at a Catholic school in Baltimore.

He tried other forms of art. One effort was a staged presentation of living Madonnas. He selected six European Madonna masterpieces to replicate. Live people would reproduce each painting on stage. Great attention was given to costume, color, background elements, and lighting in order to reproduce what was in the painting as exactly as possible. One at a time, behind a nine-by-five-foot frame, a life-sized version of the painting was presented, with a period of silence between each one. "Ave Maria" was played for each display.

Creativity was Thurman's strength, and the service was a great success. He commented, "The congregation and the participants were fused in a single moment of spiritual transcendence. I discovered, again through worship, that an experience of unity among peoples can be more compelling than all that separates and divides."[8] This was another form of mystical awareness.

In 1935, the World Christian Student Federation asked Thurman to chair a delegation of African Americans to make a pilgrimage of friendship as guests of the Student Christian Movements of India, Burma, and Ceylon. The delegation would consist of Thurman, his wife, and another African American minister, Rev. Edward Carroll, and his wife, Phenola. There was some difficulty in securing visas from Great Britain. A representative of the British government said, "If an American educated Negro just traveled through the country as a tourist, his presence would create many difficulties for our rule—now you are asking us to let four of them travel all over the country and make speeches."[9] However, the visas were issued. On this trip Thurman would engage in very serious religious and theological conversations that would reveal more of Thurman's spiritual growth.

The first stop was Ceylon, now known as Sri Lanka. In his book *Jesus and the Disinherited*, Thurman described what happened after delivering a lecture at the Law College. The principal of the college invited him into his office for coffee. As they sipped their coffee in the principal's impressive office, he wanted to know why Thurman was making this trip. He reminded him that three hundred years ago Thurman's forefathers were captured and taken from the west coast of Africa as slaves. He said, "The people who dealt in the slave trade were Christians. The men who bought slaves were Christians. Christian ministers quoting the Christian apostle Paul gave the sanction of religion to slavery. You have lived in a Christian nation in which you were segregated, lynched, and burned. Even in the church there is segregation."[10] The man told Thurman that he just could not understand how he could be such a traitor to the dark people of the earth. He challenged Thurman to defend himself. The conversation lasted over five hours.

Thurman told the man that he was not there to defend "a declining and disgraced Christian faith." He made a distinction between Christianity and the religion of Jesus. His own critique of slavery and racial prejudice was more devastating than that of his host. He also told the principal that there was a minority of people in the United States who saw in the spirit of Jesus freedom, liberty, and justice for all people. The conversation was tense, and Thurman was anxious to move on.

The delegation traveled on to India. One of Thurman's memorable encounters was with the head of the Division of Oriental Studies at an Indian university. For a morning they had a conversation about the life of the spirit in Hinduism, Buddhism, and Christianity. As Thurman got up to leave to meet some students, the man said to him, "I see you are chuckling," and Thurman noticed the same in the other man. Thurman suggested that they were laughing at the same thing. He said, "We had spent the entire morning sparring for position—you from your Hindu breastwork and I from behind my Christian embattlement." The man replied, "You are right. When we come back this afternoon let us be wiser than that."

"That afternoon," Thurman wrote, "I had the most primary, naked fusing of total religious experience with another human being of which I have ever been capable. It was as if we had stepped out of social, political, and cultural frames of reference, and allowed two human spirits to unite on a ground of reality that was unmarked by separateness and differences. This was a watershed experience in my life. We had become part of each other even as we remained essentially individual." Sharing religious faith at such a profound level bound them together spiritually in a way neither man expected.[11]

One of the high points of the trip was a meeting with Gandhi. Thurman and his wife were taken to an open field where there was a bungalow tent over which flew a flag of the Indian National Congress. Gandhi emerged from the tent to greet them, after which they were escorted to a large room in the center of the tent where they were invited to sit on the floor. They spent three hours together. Gandhi raised many questions about the racial situation in America. He asked about voting rights, lynching, discrimination, public school education, the churches and how they functioned. Thurman asked Gandhi what he thought was the greatest obstacle to Jesus Christ in India. Gandhi replied, "Christianity as it is practiced has been identified with Western culture, with Western civilization, and colonialism. This is the greatest enemy that Jesus Christ has in my country, Christianity itself."[12] There is a well-known story about a journalist asking Gandhi what he thought about Western civilization. Gandhi replied that it would be a good idea. He believed that one's religion must be able to change society, and the American churches had not yet accomplished that.

In 1945, Thurman received a letter from a Presbyterian minister in San Francisco who had a desire to develop what would become an intentionally intercultural church made up of whites, blacks, Asians, and Latinos, where everyone would be equal and participate together in all aspects of the church. He wanted Howard Thurman to be the minister.

After much deliberation with his family, Thurman decided to take the position. The church would be called the Church for the Fellowship of All Peoples. Thurman thought that here he could put to the test the major concerns of his life. Is the worship of God the central and most significant act of the human spirit? It is really true that in the presence of God there is neither male nor female, child nor adult, rich nor poor, nor any classification by which humanity defines itself in categories? Is it only in religious experience that the individual discovers what one ultimately amounts to?

At a dinner in his honor as his time at Howard University came to a close, the featured speaker was Eleanor Roosevelt. She became an associate member of Thurman's new church, as did others who lived far away from San Francisco.

Worship would be the keystone of this new church. Thurman again unleashed his creativity in making use of the arts. People began to be drawn to the church. It attracted social radicals, union members and leaders, people of the arts, and ordinary citizens. On one occasion, he was invited to give an opening prayer at a meeting of the Cooks and Stewards Union. When he finished, the president of the union walked over, shook his hand, and said, "Hell, that was good!"

The church offered intercultural workshops for children to teach them about other cultures. One little boy, having just come home from one, said to his mother, "I knew Jesus was a Baptist, but I never knew he was a Jew."

After ten years at Fellowship Church, Thurman accepted an invitation to become dean of the chapel and professor of spiritual disciplines at Boston University. He was promised a free hand to develop the chapel program as he wished. In explaining his reason for leaving the church he told the congregation, "To develop a congregation somewhat like this in a university community is to touch at every step of the way hundreds of young people who themselves will be going to the ends of the earth to take up their responsibilities as members of communities. This means the widest possible dissemination of the ideas in which I believe."[13]

LONGING FOR GOD

On his first Sunday at the University, Thurman stated in the worship bulletin:

> The Sunday morning worship service is so designed as to address itself to the deepest needs and aspirations of the human spirit. In so doing, it does not seek to undermine whatever may be the religious context which gives meaning to your particular life, but rather to deepen the authentic lines along which your quest for spiritual reality has led you. It is our hope that you will come to the Chapel not only as a place of stimulation, challenge, and dedication, but also as a symbol of the intent of the University to recognize religion as fundamental to the human enterprise.[14]

Attendance began to grow. Students from the University, as well as other schools in the area, appeared. People with no connection to any university attended. In time these people wanted to have their own church board, but the University trustees refused, fearing they would lose control. Thurman eventually resigned as dean of the chapel and became university minister at large.

Upon his retirement, he was presented with a check for $10,000 to begin the Howard Thurman Foundation to provide help for African American students. The family settled back into life in San Francisco, where he did much of his writing and his books continued to be published.

In his autobiography, Thurman defined religious experience as "a dynamic encounter between [humanity] and God."[15] He hoped that such an encounter would occur in a service of worship, when God might appear in the head, heart, and soul of the worshiper. In his book *The Creative Encounter*, he saw religious experience as "the conscious and direct exposure of the individual to God."[16] The central fact of such an experience is "the awareness of meeting God." He wrote, "Descriptive words used are varied: sometimes it is called an encounter; sometimes, a confrontation; and sometimes, a sense of Presence. The individual is seen as being exposed to direct knowledge of ultimate meaning."[17]

One of the perennial questions about religious experience is whether it is something we can generate on our own or just happens for no apparent reason. Thurman did not specifically answer that question, but he did say, "In any wilderness one may come upon a burning bush and realize that he or she is standing on holy ground." He believed in a readying process, which for him was prayer. The best preparation was the reading of Scripture, especially the Psalms and Gospels. When we are well-prepared, things happen. The initiative is in God's hands, not ours. We begin to move toward God, and God's touch of both spirit and will generates a new character in us. The whole experience involves our finding God and God finding us. In a religious experience, we see ourselves from another point of view. What do we learn about God? For Thurman, the most important learning is that God is. This, he said, is not an inference; it is a disclosure. "The firsthand knowledge of God is always a revelation. It is awareness of a literal truth directly perceived. This is the testimony of religious experience."[18]

How do we know we are not being deceived by what we think is a religious experience? To answer that question, we need to ask ourselves whether it has made any difference in who we are, in the way we live. For Thurman, a true encounter with God gives us a new focal point in life, leading us to surrender to God. He wrote, "The central surrender of the center and the slow moral conquest of the self is the struggle to carry the 'transfer of title' from the center to the outlying districts of the self." We have all experienced cycles in our religious lives when our faith alternates between deep certainty and confused questioning. "Falling and rising is the way," said Thurman, but there is in our center a light that brings us back. The surrendering of the self gives us a core purpose for living that goes beyond our private desires and personal risks. This surrender releases new energies and powers.

Thurman's book *Disciplines of the Spirit* was based on a course he taught at Boston University. His purpose in the course was to use what he called the "raw material" of daily experiences as the context for an encounter with God, because of his certainty that any experience could be the context for spiritual awareness and insight.[19]

The course was a two-semester effort. The first semester was devoted to a study of religious experience, especially Christian religious experience. The second semester consisted of a study of suffering, tragedy, and love through which a person may be ushered into the presence of God. This requires deep commitment and takes time to develop. Thurman said that "yielding to the center" may be a silent, slow process. The transformation of one's life may be so gradual until suddenly things are seen in a different light. He wrote, "Something that used to be difficult is now easier; some things that seemed all right are no longer possible. There has been a slow invasion of the Spirit of God that marked no place or time." The secret, if there is one, is "to be able to will one thing," to organize one's life around a single purpose. At the end of *The Creative Encounter*, Thurman wrote, "It is my belief that in the Presence of God there is neither male nor female, white nor black, Gentile nor Jew, Protestant nor Catholic, Hindu, Buddhist, nor [Muslim], but a human stripped to the literal substance of itself before God." Searching for this is a lifetime spiritual adventure.

Howard Thurman was a determined man. As a boy in a segregated city that did not have a high school for African Americans, he was determined to get an education and make something of himself. A few angels along the way helped. He attended Morehouse College in Atlanta, but during two summers, he took courses at Columbia University in New York. He entered a theological seminary that only admitted two African Americans a year.

A chance reading of a book by Rufus Jones led him to Haverford College to study with Jones for a semester, where he was greatly stimulated by a seminar on Meister Eckhart.

Teaching stints at Morehouse, Howard University, and Boston University; a trip to India, Burma, and Ceylon; and All Peoples' Church in California, provided opportunities for Thurman to continue to grow and develop. His use of the arts in public worship attracted many. His efforts at an intercultural church expanded his experience.

Howard Thurman's life was one of determination and innovation—his use of the arts in worship, his leadership in an intentional intercultural church, and his teaching college students. He was always ready to cross boundaries and do something new. He told us to look for that burning bush that may surprise us, but God does the unexpected. Keep learning and probing, and we will come to find God's presence in our lives.

FURTHER READING

Thurman, Howard. *The Centering Moment*. New York: Harper & Row, 1969.

———. *Essential Writings*. Edited by Luther E. Smith Jr. Modern Spiritual Masters. Maryknoll, NY: Orbis Books, 2006.

———. *With Head and Heart: The Autobiography of Howard Thurman*. New York: Harcourt Brace Jovanovich, 1979.

10

SIMONE WEIL

1906–1943
Activist Mystic

The machine broke again. How could she do her work with these continual breakdowns? This meant she would not "make the rate," her production quota for the day, and there would be little pay this week. She was making small parts for electrical equipment, and now she must wait for someone to fix the machine. She had wanted to experience the lot of the factory worker, but whatever idealism she originally had about this experience soon dissipated. The work was hot and the factory a dark, miserable place.

Sometimes her fingertips bled from the work, and she had to stand next to a very loud machine that went on all day. The noise was deafening and her ears felt numb. It was dehumanizing, and she felt anonymous in the mass of workers, crushed by fatigue, a beast of burden. There was constant pressure to produce or be fired, and her supervisors spoke in curt, harsh tones. They didn't care about anyone. There were no unions to protect the workers, no safety rules, no health insurance, no grievance procedure. The people were just cogs in the wheels of an impersonal machine that ground on, mindless of those desperate enough for a job to work there.[1]

This was France in the 1930s, the years of the Great Depression, and this factory worker was Simone Weil, daughter of a wealthy Parisian physician. I was introduced to her writings by a Trappist monk at a small, experimental monastery in rural North Carolina. She was new to me. Around that time, I was doing research at the Duke University library. On a break one afternoon, I walked across the quadrangle to the Gothic Bookstore where I saw an entire shelf of books by Weil, many of which I bought. At that time, I was working on a book on the spirituality of social activists and she looked like a good candidate to study. Her books were a treasure, and I began to read seriously this remarkable woman. Her thinking fit right in with other people I was studying on that topic.[2] She was an excellent example of someone who combined a commitment to social justice and a deep search for the presence of God in her life.

I found her interesting, sometimes even inspirational. Her evolution from activist to mystic was fascinating. Had I known her personally, however, I am not sure I would have liked her. T. S. Eliot described her as a "difficult, violent, and complex personality," yet "one who might have become a saint." Andre Gide saw her as "the most spiritual writer" of the century. Albert Camus called her "the only great spirit of our time."[3] I see her as one who fit right into the tradition of Christian mysticism, but in a somewhat unorthodox way.

Simone Weil was born on February 3, 1906, in Paris, France, the second child of an affluent family. Her birth was one month premature, and she had a sickly infancy and early childhood. Her mother breastfed her while recovering from an appendectomy. When she was weaned, she refused to eat with a spoon and had eating problems all her life. She once speculated that she had been poisoned by her mother's milk, and that explained why she thought she was such a failure. Most people who have read her writings would hardly use failure as a word to describe her. She was a brilliant mind.

Although the Weils were Jewish, they were basically agnostic and did not practice their ancestral faith. Some of the relatives did, but Simone received no formal training in religion. She saw herself as French rather than Jewish, though she would later suffer under Nazism because of her ethnic background.

As Simone and her brother, Andre, were growing up, all toys and dolls were banned from the home by their mother, who believed such trifles hindered intellectual development. Andre was solving advanced mathematical problems by age nine, by twelve he had taught himself classical Greek and Sanskrit and had developed skill in playing the violin. He became a mathematical prodigy and would later in life join the Institute for Advanced Studies at Princeton.

Simone was a bit slower, but she was reading the newspaper to her family by age five. In her early teens, she mastered Greek and several modern languages. The children often communicated with each other in Greek or in rhymed couplets. Simone once told Andre that she had completed a Latin composition and was now ready to study Aeschylus with him.

Their mother, Selma Weil, took charge of their education and planned every element of their intellectual development. She was also concerned about their physical development and had a great dread of germs—she did not want her children to be kissed by anyone outside the family and imposed a regimen of compulsive handwashing. For the rest of her life Simone was repulsed by any kind of physical contact with other people.

She was greatly offended by a remark of a family friend who implied that she had the good looks and Andre had the brains. In response, she suppressed her femininity and was determined to develop herself intellectually. In time she learned how to argue brilliantly and dress unattractively, leading some people to call her "the categorical imperative in skirts."[4]

Simone Weil

When war broke out in 1914, Dr. Weil was called into the French army, and the family followed him wherever it was practical. It was then that Weil began to exhibit her desire to identify with human suffering. She refused to eat sugar as long as French soldiers at the front were deprived of it, and throughout her life she would deny herself what the most unfortunate people did not have.

In 1919, she entered the Lycee Fenelon, a public high school and junior college for girls, but in 1923, she went through a spiritual crisis that nearly ended in suicide. She was overwhelmed by a sense of complete unworthiness by comparison with her genius brother and suffered almost unbearable headaches. Later, she would say that "to know one is mediocre is to be 'on the way.'" Somehow, she recovered. Although she failed by her own standards, she always pleased her teachers.

In 1924, she began studies in philosophy at the Lycee Victor Duruy. After graduation she became a student at the Lycee Henri IV, one of the first women to be admitted. There she was a student of an important French philosopher, Emile-Auguste Chartier, who wrote under the name Alain. This study helped her to place first in the entrance examinations to the École Normale Supérieure—immediately ahead of the only other woman student, Simone de Beauvoir, whose book, *The Second Sex*, would help launch the feminist movement twenty years later.

Weil's intellectual interests were wide ranging. She studied Greek, Latin, Sanskrit, modern languages, philosophy, Western and Eastern religions, mathematics, science, and literature. She developed an interest in Marxism, which she would later denounce, as well as pacifism and trade unionism. In 1931, at age twenty-two, she received her degree in philosophy with the thesis *Science and Perception in Descartes*.

Her first teaching post was in Le Puy, an obscure village. She had wanted to be in a large city or port, but the education authorities wanted her out of the way. They found her views on Marxism, unions, pacifism, and the state of the poor too controversial. She gave her surplus food to the poor and marched in picket lines. Her mother, wanting to help establish her new life, found an apartment and furnished it for her. Weil did not like her parents taking care of her, but they were always there when she was in trouble. Later, she got rid of most of the furniture and lived with the bare minimum, showing no interest in material things, a mystery to her affluent parents.

During school hours, she taught philosophy; the rest of the time was spent in marches with unemployed workers and advocating for the poor. At a demonstration, her detractors called her "the Red Virgin of the tribe of Levi."[5] Mark Gibbard described her as "an earnest and committed radical, though one who never joined a political party."[6] The superintendent for instruction became disturbed at her radical activity and threatened to withdraw her license to teach. Simone told him that she would consider such an event as "the crown of her career." He did not follow through on the threat, and she transferred to Auxerre for the next school year. Her students did not do well on exams, so the school abolished the philosophy position.

Her next post was at Roanne. Here she was known as a communist and an atheist, although she was neither in the strict sense of those terms. Advocates for social justice are often under suspicion because of people's natural resistance to change. She did participate in a miners' march, protesting wage reductions and unemployment.

She wanted to experience the lot of the factory worker, complaining that many theoretical Marxists never did. Taking a leave of absence from teaching in 1934–35, she found a job in a factory. She left an account of her experience in a journal, published as "Factory Journal." Her frustration with machines that broke down or did not work properly always cost her production time. One of the persistent entries in her journal was "didn't make the rate," the production quota for full pay.

Entry after entry described her suffering. "The speed is dizzying," she wrote, "especially when, in order to throw yourself into it you had to overcome fatigue, headache, and the feeling of being fed up." Later she entered,

> I came near to being broken. I almost was—my courage, the feeling that I had value as a person were nearly broken during a period I would be humiliated to remember...I got up in the mornings with anguish. I went to the factory with dread; I worked like a slave, the noon break was a wrenching experience; I got back to my place at 5:45, preoccupied immediately with getting enough sleep...and with waking up early enough....The feeling of self-respect, such as it has been built up by society, is destroyed.[7]

Many years later, in her spiritual autobiography, *Waiting for God*, she described how factory work had helped her identify with the suffering of others. "As I worked in the factory, indistinguishable from all eyes, including my own, from the anonymous mass, the affliction of others entered into my flesh and my soul. Nothing separated me from it."[8] Her identification with the poor was intense.

Her parents came to her rescue and took her on a trip to Spain and Portugal to nurse her back to health. On this trip, the first of three important religious experiences took place, which moved her toward Christian faith. Wanting some time alone, she went to a small Portuguese fishing village on the day of the festival of its patron saint. She watched the wives of the fishermen process by the boats, carrying candles and singing what she believed to be "very ancient hymns of heartbreaking sadness." She said, "There the conviction was suddenly borne upon me that Christianity is pre-eminently the religion of slaves, that slaves cannot help belonging to it, and I among others."[9] Her identification with the poor and unemployed gave her a view of life far different from her early life of Parisian affluence. Where religion had no importance for her in that context, now she saw reality in a very different way and appreciated the value of religious traditions among the poor. It gave hope and meaning to their lives. For Weil, an opening to faith began to develop.

After her recovery, she taught at Bourges for the 1935–36 school year. She gave away most of her salary and continued her radical activity. Although her teaching methods were unorthodox, this time her students did well on examinations. It was her most successful year of teaching.

In 1936, her concern for justice drew her into the Spanish Civil War on the side of anarchists fighting Franco's fascists. Since she was a pacifist, she was made a cook for the camp. Her usual ineptness betrayed her when she accidentally stepped into a pot of boiling oil and severely burned a leg. That ended the Spanish adventure, which was fortunate since her unit was soon wiped out.

Once again, her parents came to the rescue, taking her on vacations to Switzerland and Italy. It was on this trip that a second major experience occurred that moved her toward Christianity. In 1937, she spent what she called "two marvelous days" in Assisi, Italy, which included a visit to the chapel where St. Francis had prayed. There, she said, "something stronger than I was compelled me for the first time...to go down on my knees."[10] A hidden Christian piety was beginning to emerge.

She tried teaching again, this time at Saint-Quentin near Paris, but persistent and painful headaches made her life an agony, forcing her to end her teaching career.

In the spring of 1938, she had a third important experience. She spent ten days at the Abbey of Solesmes and attended all the Easter liturgy, captivated by the Gregorian chant for which the Abbey was famous. It was here that a decisive experience occurred. She wrote,

Simone Weil

> I was suffering from splitting headaches; each sound hurt me like a blow; by an extreme effort of concentration I was able to rise above this wretched flesh, to leave it to suffer by itself, heaped up in corner; and to find a pure and perfect joy in the unimaginable beauty of the chanting and the words. This experience enabled me by analogy to get a better understanding of the possibility of loving divine love in the midst of affliction. It goes without saying that in the course of these services the thought of the Passion of Christ entered into my being once and for all.[11]

In identifying with the suffering of Christ she found new meaning in her own pain. As Christ continued to love, she began to find the possibility of loving God while suffering.

While at Solesmes, she met a young English Catholic who introduced her to George Herbert's poem "Love." The poem delighted her, so she learned it by heart and recited it as a prayer when her headaches were at their worst. It was during a recitation of this poem that she had her first mystical experience. She said, "Christ came down and took possession of me." For the first time she realized that it was possible for humans to have contact with the Divine. Now, she said, when Christ possessed her "neither my senses nor my imagination had any part. I only felt in the midst of my suffering the presence of love."[12] From now on her religious feelings would dominate her thought, although there would be no lessening of her social concern.

After the German occupation of Paris, the Weil family moved to Marseilles, where her mystical life intensified. In 1940, she was officially dismissed by the state teaching service under the Vichy anti-Jewish laws. She soon met Father J. M. Perrin and developed a deep friendship. He became her spiritual director. He eventually sent her to Gustave Thibon, a lay theologian who operated a Catholic agricultural colony in Southern France.

Thibon resisted Weil, believing that intellectuals, especially philosophy graduates, were incapable of prolonged manual work. But Father Perrin insisted, and Thibon's sympathy for persecuted Jews caused him to accept her.

He described Simone Weil in his introduction to her book *Gravity and Grace*. "She was just beginning to open with all her soul to Christianity; a limpid mysticism emanated from her; in no other human being have I come across such familiarity with religious mysteries; never have I felt the word *supernatural* to be more charged with reality than when in contact with her." Her argumentative nature was a problem, but Thibon handled it with patience, and he regarded her teaching as "educative genius." He praised her for teaching him about Plato, whom she regarded as a mystic.[13]

On May 17, 1942, the Weil family sailed for the United States, where it would take an apartment on Riverside Drive in New York. Simone, as we would expect, was unhappy in America. She found the life too secure and could not endure it, knowing how the French suffered from Nazism and war. At the same time, she attended daily Mass at Corpus Christi Church on 121st Street, the church where Thomas Merton had been baptized.

She learned that her desire to be parachuted back into France was unrealistic, which made returning out of the question. Still, she was determined to join the French Resistance. On November 9, 1942, she left her family and sailed for England, where she would work for the Free French government in exile. Here she wrote her book *The Need for Roots*, which outlined her ideas for the development of postwar France. It was not actually published until 1949, six years after her death.

The Need for Roots has three parts. Part 1 is "The Needs of the Soul," which include order, liberty, responsibility, equality, freedom of opinion, security, private property, and truth. Part 2 is "Uprootedness," which described losses produced by war, such as unemployment, the loss of a national culture, and other factors.

Part 3 is "The Growing of Roots." She said, "To be rooted is perhaps the most important and least recognized need of the human soul."[14] In his preface, T. S. Eliot wrote that this book "ought to be studied by the young before their leisure is lost and their capacity for thought is lost."[15]

Simone Weil believed that human nature was controlled by forces external to individuals, specifically a spiritual gravity, and the only hope for beneficial change was to be found in the grace of God. In her book *Gravity and Grace*, a collection of items from her notebooks put together by Gustave Thibon, she said, "All the natural movements of the soul are controlled by laws analogous to those of physical gravity." Grace is the only exception. We must always expect things to happen in uniformity with the laws of gravity, unless there is supernatural intervention.[16]

Gravity draws us down to the lowest level of living. She believed this because of her own experience. It is gravity that encourages us to do evil to others. She wrote, "I must not forget that at certain times when my headaches were raging, I had an intense longing to make another human being suffer by hitting him in exactly the same part of his forehead. When in this state I have several times succumbed to the temptation at least to say words that caused pain. Obedience to the force of gravity [is] the greatest sin."[17]

Gravity and Grace has an aphoristic character about it. We find such statements as the following: "Creation is composed to descending movements of gravity [and] the ascending movements of grace." Human nature causes us to fall; grace causes us to rise. We have already encountered this notion in the thinking of Plotinus. In our spiritual lives we go through cycles of falling and rising. A different kind of movement is described in another aphorism: "To lower oneself is to rise in the domain of moral gravity. Moral gravity makes us fall to the heights."[18] Weil believed that the more she identified with those at the lower level of society, the higher she would rise toward God.

LONGING FOR GOD

It is important, she believed, for people to recognize their limitations. It is essential "to grasp that there is a limit, and, without supernatural help, that limit cannot be passed." People need to face up to their realities about the world and themselves. "I am other than what I imagine myself to be," she wrote. "To know this is forgiveness."[19]

For Simone Weil, truth was to be found more in suffering than in pleasure. She said, "It is human misery and not pleasure which contains the secret of divine wisdom. All pleasure-seeking is the search for an artificial paradise, an intoxication, an enlargement. But it gives us nothing except the experience that it is vain. Only the contemplation of our limitations...puts us on a higher plane. 'Whosoever humbleth himself shall be exalted.'"[20] For Weil, the reason for believing in God's mercy was her mystical experience. She said, "Those who have had the privilege of mystical contemplation [have] experienced the mercy of God. That is why mysticism is the only source of virtue for humanity. Because when [people] do not believe that there is infinite mercy behind the curtain of the world...they become cruel."[21]

The experiences in Portugal, and in Assisi and Solesmes, created within her an openness to God, but her mystical life steadily deepened around the recitation of the Our Father. She and a friend decided to learn it by heart in Greek, the language in which it was first written. Gradually, she developed the practice of saying it each morning "with absolute attention." If her attention wandered or failed, she would begin again until she succeeded in going through it with absolutely pure attention. She tells of what happened when she was able to do it:

> At times the very first words tear my thoughts from my body and transport it to a place where there is neither perspective nor point of view. The infinity of the ordinary expanses of perception is replaced by an infinity to the second or sometimes the third degree. At the

same time, filling every part of this infinity, there is a silence, a silence which is not an absence of sound but which is an object of positive sensation, more positive than that of sound. Noises, if there are any, only reach me after crossing this silence. Sometimes, also, during this recitation or at other moments, Christ is present with me in person, but his presence is infinitely more real, more moving, more clear than on that first occasion when he took possession of me.[22]

This led her to understand perfect prayer as perfect attention. She wrote a fascinating essay titled, "Reflection on the Right Use of School Studies with a View to the Love of God." Weil began the essay, "The key to the Christian conception of studies is the realization that prayer consists of attention. It is the orientation of all the attention of which the soul is capable toward God. This orientation accounts for much of the quality of prayer. Warmth of heart cannot make up for it."[23]

School studies, she believed, teach us how to focus our attention. It does not matter what the subject is. It could be mathematics, geometry, a foreign language, creative writing, or anything else. They all require that we concentrate our attention. We may spend hours trying to solve a problem in geometry and not succeed. Nevertheless, the time has not been wasted. She said, "We have been making progress each minute of that hour in another mysterious dimension. Without our knowing or feeling it, this apparently barren effort has brought more light into the soul. The result one day will be discovered in prayer."

At this point in her life, Simone Weil had never been baptized although she had a great love for Catholicism. She said, "I love God, Christ, and the Catholic faith as much as it is possible for so miserably an inadequate creature to love them. I love the saints through their writings and what is told of their lives. I love the six or seven Catholics of genuine spirituality whom chance has led me to meet in the course of my life. I love the Catholic liturgy, hymns, architecture, rites, and ceremonies."[24]

She had a strange belief that God did not want her in the Church. Her internal resistance was the work of God in her. She did not want the Church to tell her what she should believe, as well as what she should not read. She was a free spirit and that was part of her greatness. Weil had a deep sense of exile. She simply did not fit in with the world. She said in a letter, "I feel that it is necessary and ordained that I should be alone, a stranger and exile in relation to every human circle without exception."[25] Only in this way, she felt, could she be her true self.

She feared that the Church would put too many intellectual restrictions on her, and she could never abide that. In *Conjectures of a Guilty Bystander*, Thomas Merton wrote of "Simone Weil, who preferred not to be in the middle of that Catholically-approved and well-censored page, but only on the margin."[26] She had a deep faith in Christ, whom she mystically encountered, and that towered above all the concerns of the institutional Church.

Although she resisted baptism, her faith ultimately determined who she was. The combination of social commitment and the encounter with Christ produced a remarkable woman whose life exemplified some of the best in the Christian tradition. In many ways her life was an authentic imitation of Christ in her identification with suffering and the poor. This, she believed, brought her into contact with the mercy of God.

While working with the Free French, Simone Weil refused to eat more than the rations allowed in France during the war. Weakened by hunger, she was forced to enter a hospital, where she suffered because of special attention given to her. She had a horror of privilege, and only felt at ease on the lowest rung of the social ladder, lost among the poor and the outcasts of the world. It was in that context that she discovered Christ.

After a few weeks in the hospital, she asked for a priest. The chaplain of the Free French came to see her. Although she was feverish, she listed some of the reasons she opposed baptism and asked the priest about the fate of unbaptized children. The priest gave her a blessing that seemed to calm her. She told a friend, "If some day I'm completely deprived of will and in a coma, then I should be baptized."[27] A few days later, water was poured on her head and the baptism formula was pronounced.

On August 17, 1943, she was moved to Grosvenor Sanatorium in Ashford, Kent. Still refusing food, she died on August 24. The coroner's report said, "Cardiac failure due to myocardial degeneration of the heart muscles, due to starvation and pulmonary tuberculosis…the deceased did kill and slay herself by refusing to eat whilst the balance of her mind was disturbed."[28]

Thus ended the life of a remarkable woman who combined social justice commitments with a deepening mystical life. Her parents spent their remaining days copying out all of her writings to preserve them, thus creating a significant corpus of religious literature that is still read and studied.

Simone Weil is remembered today as one of the great intellectuals, social justice advocates, and spiritual writers of the first half of the twentieth century. Her combination of genius, mysticism, and sensitivity to the suffering of others gives her an important place in the pantheon of Christianity. She grew up in affluence but gave herself to the poor. She loved the Catholic tradition but refused to be part of the Church. She had a deep appreciation for Eastern religions, particularly the Hinduism of the Upanishads and the Bhagavad Gita. She loved languages and wanted to translate the classics for other people. To study her life is to be overwhelmed by her intellect, faith, and commitments to humanity. Yet, she lived simply and humbly, more comfortable at the lowest levels of society. Her knowledge, her activism, her wide-ranging interest, and the depth of her religious experience will be read and studied for many years to come.

Simone Weil's spiritual quest was long, difficult, and painful. She was a free spirit. Growing up in a family with no real

LONGING FOR GOD

religious interest, she studied many religions but committed to none. Throughout her life, she identified with poor, suffering, and underprivileged people. She gave away much of what she had, and she marched in demonstrations with unemployed persons. She participated in the Spanish Civil War because she identified with the plight of those who were opposing fascism. She observed poor families in a religious procession for the patron saints of their community and drew spiritual insight into her own human condition. She constantly refused help from her parents.

All of this was a prelude to spiritual breakthrough. No matter who we are, we all need to examine carefully our own preludes. What in our past might have led to a deeper desire for God? Simone took all of those experiences with her when she visited a monastery known for the high quality of their Latin chant, which moved her deeply. A visit to the chapel of St. Francis in Assisi led to her first experience of prayer. Conversations with others deepened her understanding of faith. Weil never gave up her concern for poor people or those living under the Nazi regime, or for France itself—how it would be following German occupation. Faith and action were united in Simone Weil, and they can be united in us.

FURTHER READING

Coles, Robert. *Simone Weil: A Modern Pilgrimage*. Reading, MA: Addison-Wesley, 1987.
Du Plessix Gray, Francine. *Simone Weil*. Penguin *Lives*. New York: Penguin Putnam, 2001.
Weil, Simone. *Waiting for God*. Translated by Emma Craufurd. New York: HarperCollins, 2009.

11

DOROTHY DAY

1897–1980
A Harsh and Dreadful Love

They were lined up outside the door: unemployed, homeless, alcoholic, addicted, mentally ill, misfit. They were looking for a bowl of soup and a hot cup of coffee. These were Dorothy Day's people, poor and troubled. She lived in poverty herself, a choice she had made long ago when she founded an organization to take care of as many of them as possible. The work was hard. There was never enough money to meet expenses, to feed them all. The volunteer staff often had to break up fights. Sometimes it all became too much for her—occasionally, she had to get away for a while. But she always came back.

Hers was a different kind of mysticism. She saw no lights, had no sense of union with God. No visions came to her. But she was sure that she saw God in those people lined up outside. She went to Mass daily, prayed the psalms, and read theologians. Her Catholic faith sustained her even though the Church—that is, the bishops and other officials—was suspicious of her. She could be a thorn in the flesh to many because of her pacifism, her sense of justice, and her criticisms of capitalism. Some saw her as a candidate for sainthood, but she would never agree to that. She said calling a person a saint is the way people try to dismiss someone.

Dorothy Day was born in Brooklyn, New York, in 1897. Her father's family was of Scottish-Irish ancestry from Tennessee and had fought for the Confederacy during the Civil War. Her mother's family had English roots; from upstate New York, they had fought for the Union.

When Day was eight, the family moved to Oakland, California, just in time for the San Francisco earthquake. The human suffering she saw had a significant impact on her. People were homeless, they had lost everything. Family members had disappeared. The scenes of destruction were horrible. She saw great pain, but also human kindness and warmth. People tried to help each other. Dorothy's mother and neighbors worked all day cooking hot meals. People gave generously, and while the crisis lasted, they loved each other. She later wrote, "It makes one think of how people could, if they would, care for each other in times of stress, ungrudgingly, with pity and with love."[1]

After that catastrophe, the family moved to Chicago to try to start a new life. Her father, a journalist, attempted to write fiction. This was the first time Day's family was actually poor. They lived in an apartment over a store on Cottage Avenue. There was no backyard or grass, only pavement. To get away, Dorothy would often walk down to Lake Michigan.

The Day family was not religious, but an incident occurred in Chicago that profoundly affected the young Dorothy. One day, she went to visit a friend and, thinking the girl was home, she entered the house only to find her friend's mother, Mrs. Barrett, on her knees praying. She told Dorothy that her friend had gone out, and resumed her prayers. Day later wrote that she felt a burst of love toward Mrs. Barrett that she never forgot. This woman had God, and in the midst of poverty, she found joy and beauty in her life. The combination of the earthquake experience and living in poverty herself generated in Day a growing sensitivity to poor people, injustice, and oppression. There were moments, however, in the midst of terrible situations, when life could be "shot through with glory"—Mrs. Barrett, in her poor little home, finished her breakfast dishes and fell down on her knees and prayed.

Dorothy Day's developing social conscience was fed in high school when she read widely on her own and was influenced by Dostoyevsky, Tolstoy, and Kropotkin. She became interested in American radicalism and loved the novels of Jack London and Upton Sinclair, who wrote about human suffering in a variety of situations.

Later, during the Depression, she would see disabled people, some missing arms and legs, some blind and exhausted by industrialism. She saw farmers overloaded with debt and impoverished mothers with hungry children clinging to their skirts. She felt a calling to help these people but did not know what do. She wondered where the saints were to try to change the social order. The religion she saw practiced in America had no vitality to it. It was a matter of Sunday praying, not everyday life. Christ was two thousand years dead and there were no prophets taking his place. She wanted churches to deal with the issues of poverty, social injustice, and human suffering that she saw all around her.

During her sophomore year in college, Day's family moved back to New York, and her father, having not succeeded as a novelist, resumed his journalistic career. He was a sports writer, and that was his first love. Dorothy, still at the university and beginning to feel homesick, decided to rejoin her family. She dropped out of school and tried to find work as a journalist. Her father did not think it was a proper occupation for a woman and told all the editors he knew not to hire her.

Eventually, she found work as a writer for radical newspapers. First, she wrote for *The Call*, a socialist paper, and later for

LONGING FOR GOD

The Masses, described by one writer as "the most exciting little radical magazine of the day."[2] Her circle of friends included the preeminent American communists of their day: Emma Goldman, Max Eastman, and John Reed, and all of whom were excited about the Communist revolution. Others were leftist intellectuals, and Day soon reconstructed her life around all-night discussions of social issues in Greenwich Village taverns.

When *The Masses* was closed down by the federal government under the 1917 Espionage Act, the newly unemployed Day went to Washington to picket in front of the White House for women's suffrage. She was arrested and served a thirty-day jail sentence, which she described as one of the major trials of her life. The first six days in prison seemed like six thousand years. In her autobiography, *The Long Loneliness*, she wrote, "I lost all consciousness of any cause. I had no sense of being a radical, making a protest against the government, carrying on a nonviolent revolution. I could only feel darkness and isolation all around me. I would never be free again, never free when I know that behind bars all over the world there are women and men, young girls and boys, suffering constraint, punishment, isolation and hardship for crimes of which all of us were guilty."[3]

While in prison, Day asked for a Bible and read it as long as there was light. The cell was dismal, dark gray walls with the dirt of the ages. The smell of unwashed prisoners was overwhelming. It was difficult to read in the fading light. She had rejected religion, but in the hopelessness of that cell, she fell back on religious instincts she had as a child. The reading, however, was of no great help. At that moment she could not foresee how important faith would be to her later in life. She felt an intense conflict between her desire to read the Bible and her pride, which did not want to go to God "in defeat and sorrow." She prayed but did not really know what she prayed.

When released, she returned to New York and joined the staff of *The Liberator*, another left-wing paper, the successor to

The Masses. She was now well-established as a part of the Greenwich Village literary and social avant-garde. Her friends were well-known writers: John Dos Passos, Caroline Gordon, Allen Tate, Hart Crane, and Malcom and Peggy Cowley. Day developed a relationship with Eugene O'Neill, a young playwright. They were all liberal, radical, and bohemian. But some of her leftist friends said she was too religious to be a good radical. Religious faith would put her in another world, not the one that was most important to them. It would be a distraction to the issues that energized them.

In fact, religious stirrings had begun to surface in Day. Often, after spending all night with friends in a Village bar, she would drop in St. Joseph's Catholic Church on Sixth Avenue on her way home. She sometimes attended an early morning Mass and knelt in the back of the church, not really understanding what was going on, but finding herself comforted by the candles, silence, people praying, and a general atmosphere of worship.

She decided that her life lacked real purpose, so she began nurses' training in a Brooklyn hospital. Perhaps this would be a way to serve human suffering. After several months of training, however, she concluded that this was not her calling. She wanted something more radical.

The next few years of Day's life were melancholy. She went back to Chicago, where she had an affair with a newsman, Lionel Moise, which resulted in a pregnancy and, subsequently, an abortion. Day wrote about it in her novel *The Eleventh Virgin*. Soon after Moise ended the relationship, she married Barkeley Tobey, on the rebound, as she put it. He was a strange character who seemed to have some involvement with the publishing business. He and Day went to Europe for a year, and she enjoyed living in Italy, but when they returned, she knew the marriage was over. During his life he would be married eight times. Day held a variety of jobs, including modeling for artists and working as a sales clerk.

LONGING FOR GOD

There in Chicago, she had another traumatic jail experience. While visiting a suicidal woman in a rooming house run for members of the International Workers of the World, a radical labor union, the place was raided by the police. Day and the woman were arrested, charged with prostitution, and taken to jail.

In the adjacent cell, a drug addict beat her head against the metal walls and howled like a wild animal. Her suffering was unspeakable. Day put her hands over her ears and a pillow over her head to muffle the sounds of a woman who was paying a high price for the pleasure drugs brought her. It made Day think about the disorder of the world—how the dreariness of addiction results from the first petty self-indulgence. The charges were dropped after Day and other demonstrators spent several days in jail.

Day's sister, Della, joined her in Chicago. She, too, had been radicalized, became a communist, and supported the Loyalist movement in Spain. She was tired of Chicago and wanted to move to New Orleans, so Dorothy, in the fall of 1923, joined her. Day had completed a novel that was accepted by a publisher. When the book came out, the moving picture rights were sold, netting her $2,500, which would later enable her to buy a small house on the beach in New York. Meanwhile, she wrote for the New Orleans *Item*. In the evenings she attended services at the Catholic cathedral. A friend gave her a rosary that Day used while attending Benediction services.

In 1924, Day returned to her house in New York. Many of her previous friends were no longer there, but a few were. She met Forster Batterham, whom she described as an anarchist and biologist, and with whom she entered into a common-law marriage. She wrote for *The New Masses* and experienced a brief period of happiness.

Her religious longings began to increase, much to the unhappiness of Batterham, who had no use for religion. When Day became pregnant, he became more distant. She had earlier expressed a desire for a child but feared that her Chicago abortion might make it impossible. She was very happy when Tamar Teresa was born. She decided to have the child baptized, knowing that this would end the relationship with Batterham, although they would stay in touch for the rest of their lives.

Tamar was baptized in July 1927. The impact of this on Day was very deep. She was drawn to the Church, and she was baptized in December. Those early thoughts about religion, often quickly rejected, finally came together. What appeared to be a sudden decision was actually the result of a long series of religious stirrings. The price was high—the loss of Batterham—but in her mind, it was worth it, painful as the loss was. She would become a major but highly controversial influence in the American Catholic Church.

Why Catholicism? Day believed that the Catholic Church, being an immigrant church, was the church of poor people. She was not naïve about its problems, but she said, "My very experience as a radical, my whole makeup, let me want to associate myself with others, with the masses, in loving and praising God."[4] The experiences of an earthquake, seeing religion in friends, suffering in prison, dropping into a church after all-night parties, discussions, and arguments, using the gift of a rosary, a concern that the Church be more prophetic about social issues, and motherhood, all came together.

She held a number of jobs after the breakup with Batterham. Then she was hired as a scriptwriter in Hollywood. Although she was paid every Friday, she was actually given nothing to do. She moved to Mexico City, taking Tamar with her, and wrote articles about poor people for *Commonweal*. Near the end of 1932, in the depths of the Depression, *Commonweal* sent her to Washington, D.C., to cover the hunger march of the unemployed. She was frustrated by the lack of Catholic leadership in dealing with the social problems caused by the Depression, and she prayed that some way would be found for her to help poor people.

LONGING FOR GOD

In 1939, she published a book titled *House of Hospitality* in which she commented on the hunger march. She stood on the sidewalk in Washington with many others and observed a ragged band of people, mostly men, looking for hope in the nation's capital, demonstrating their solidarity with each other. They needed food, they needed jobs, they needed agricultural prices high enough to sell crops for a living. She looked around at the prosperous people in the crowd who were there out of curiosity and mused to herself, "These are Christ's poor. He was one of them. He was a man like other men, and He chose His friends amongst the ordinary workers. These men have been betrayed by Christianity. Men are not Christian today. If they were, this sight would not be possible. Far dearer in the sight of God are these hungry, ragged ones, than all those smug, well-fed Christians who sit in their homes, cowering in fear of the communist menace."[5]

Day said that now that she was a Catholic, she could not be a Communist, but she desperately wanted to do something. She prayed that God would show her a way. That prayer would soon be answered.

When she returned to New York, she found waiting for her an energetic and talkative individual named Peter Maurin. He was a French peasant who had once belonged to the Christian Brothers order, but later joined Le Sillon, a French progressive Catholic group interested in political and social issues. Eventually, he moved to Canada and worked as a laborer, then went to New York, where he worked just long enough to provide for his physical needs. Otherwise, he spent his time reading in the New York Public Library and standing around Union Square talking to whomever would listen. During a hospital stay, Maurin listed his occupation as "agitator." He had developed a philosophy of radicalism based on Christian action but needed someone who had the talent to present his ideas to the world. An editor at *Commonweal* suggested that he contact Dorothy Day. When they finally met, a fateful encounter took place—her life would never be the same.

Maurin took it as a personal mission to develop Day's Catholic intellectual background. He gave her some of the Christian spiritual classics to read and instructed her in church history and the lives of the saints. Together they began a monthly newspaper, *The Catholic Worker*, with the objective of promoting social action based on Catholic teaching.

The first issue appeared on May 1, 1933. *The Catholic Worker* carried articles about unemployment, trade unions, cooperatives, the exploitation of black Americans, child labor, and a local strike. Maurin believed that the paper should not just report the news but also should comment on it. It was not enough, he said, to report that a man died and left an estate worth two million dollars. It must be said that he left that much because he did not know how to give to poor people for Christ's sake. The paper avoided political partisanship. Day and Maurin did not see politics as a means of social reform and they never endorsed any political party.

For the first edition, 2,500 copies were printed to sell at Union Square for a penny a copy, still the price of the paper today. The Communists were selling their paper, *The Daily Worker*, and shouting, "Read *The Daily Worker!*" Dorothy Day's people yelled back, "Read *The Catholic Worker* daily!" Circulation reached a peak of 190,000 in 1938. Numbers fell during World War II because of Day's pacifism. By 1984, it had stabilized at around 104,000. Catholics had not had that kind of publication before. It reported on what was happening to poor people and presented commentary on a variety of social issues: racism, labor, unemployment, poor housing, hunger, injustice, and, as World War II approached, war and peace.

The second major effort by Day and Maurin was to establish a House of Hospitality where poor people could find food and shelter. The stated purpose of the Catholic Worker movement was "to realize in the individual and society the expressed and implied teaching of Jesus." They wanted major changes in society but said that they must come by a pacifist approach. They were absolutely opposed to the use of violence and force as a means of social change. Day said she wanted to build a society where it would be easier for people to be good.[6]

In 1963, she made a trip to Rome that she wrote about in *The Catholic Worker*: "I came away from Rome more convinced than ever that the particular vocation of *The Catholic Worker* is to reach the man in the street, to write about the glorious truths of Christianity, the great adventures of the spirit, which can affect so great a transformation in the lives of men if they would consent to the promptings of the Spirit."[7]

Promptings of the Spirit? Here Day begins to reveal something about her spirituality. Was she a mystic like the others present in this book? Yes, but hers was not a traditional mysticism. She did have a deep interior life. She prayed regularly and attended Mass daily, but her basic experience was seeing God in other people. She based this idea on the parable of the last judgment in Matthew 25, where Christ says, "I was hungry and you gave me food, I was thirsty and you gave me something to drink, I was a stranger and you welcomed me, I was naked and you gave me clothing, I was sick and you took care of me, I was in prison and you visited me" (vv. 35–36). When the disciples asked when they did these things, Christ answered, "Just as you did it to one of the least of these…you did it to me" (v. 40). Day believed that when we do something to or for another person, we are doing it to Christ. That is where God is found.

In 1960, Day was aware that people in the peace movement thought that *The Catholic Worker* effort of taking care of poor people was like putting a Band-Aid® on cancer. But for Day it was important to care for the wounded while trying to slay the giant. "We are commanded over and over again by Jesus Christ himself to do these things," she wrote. "What we do for the least of these we do for him. We are judged by this."[8]

The primary revelation of God's presence for Dorothy Day was poor people. She said, "He is incarnate in poor people, in the bread we break together. We know him and each other in the breaking of bread."[9] It is not always easy to see the Divine in people. It is hidden and obscured to a greater or lesser degree in each of us. Those who came to the Catholic Worker house for help were often alcoholic, demented, or drug addicted. They could be hostile, sometimes violent. Day was fond of quoting a line from a Russian novel, *The Brothers Karamazov*,[10] "Love in practice is a harsh and dreadful thing compared to love in dreams." In one of her newspaper columns, she wrote, "It is hard to see the dear sweet Christ in many a pestering drunk that comes in, demanding attention. These staggering, unlovely, filthy ones who come in waving a bottle at you and cursing you…are God's messengers."

These were people, she believed, for whom Christ demanded that hospitality be given. She was convinced that when she offered food or shelter to those in need she was functioning as Lazarus or Martha or Mary, and that the guest was Christ. No haloes appeared, but that was not the way Christ was present. The Virgin Mary did not appear as a woman clothed in the sun with twelve stars on her head and the moon under her feet, whom we read about in the Book of Revelation. Such an appearance would have impressed many, Day said, but "that wasn't God's way for her nor is it Christ's way for himself now, when he is disguised under every type of humanity that treads the earth."[11]

Eventually, Catholic Worker houses opened in other American cities. The movement had enormous influence. Many college students would work at the houses in the summers. One of the early editors of *The Catholic Worker*, Michael Harrington, later wrote a landmark book, *The Other America*, which reported on

LONGING FOR GOD

a major study of poverty in America and influenced many politicians.

The syndicated columnist Gary Wills was greatly influenced by Dorothy Day. He called her one of the great figures of the twentieth century and said that when people met her they would often say to themselves, "I've got to be better than I am." Petra Kelly, the leader of Germany's Green Party, said that Day belonged in the company of Gandhi and Martin Luther King Jr.[12] Her impact on people was remarkable.

She continued to find herself in jail from time to time. She was arrested for demonstrating with Cesar Chavez's United Farm Workers during strikes. She refused to participate in civil defense drills in New York City and was arrested.

Many people who were not poor visited the Catholic Worker house to talk with Dorothy Day. In 1943, two sailors came to the house and talked with her all night long about war and peace, humanity, and the state. Later, she remembered the men were brothers, Joe and John F. Kennedy. Another frequent visitor was Father Daniel Berrigan, an antiwar leader in the Vietnam era who sometimes offered Mass at the Catholic Worker house.

Life at the Catholic Worker was marked by voluntary poverty, as the house was in a slum area of New York. Day wrote in one of her newspaper columns, "We admit we are beggars and we are not ashamed of it. We will work as hard as we can, with no salary, and trust to the Lord to care for those He sends us....So we remain in the cities, the gutter sweepers of the dioceses, working yet beggars, destitute yet possessing all things; happy because today the sun shines, there is a symphony on the radio, children are playing on the streets, there is a park across the way and a church around the corner where we receive our daily Bread."[13]

Dorothy Day's life came to an end when she was eighty-three, on the evening of November 29, 1980. She had been suffering from congestive heart failure for some time and her last years were spent confined to her room. Her work among poor, destitute, and deranged people reveals what a harsh and dreadful thing love can be. It can put one in the midst of terrible human suffering. Yet she believed that the gospel called people to that kind of love, for it is the love of Christ.

William Miller, in his fine biography of Dorothy Day, reported that a funeral procession of Day's friends and fellow Catholic Workers was led by her grandchildren carrying the pine box in which she would be buried. As the procession stopped so Cardinal Terrance Cooke could bless the body, a demented man pushed his way through the crowd and stared at the pine box intently. No one tried to stop him because it was in such people that Dorothy Day saw God.

Her life's journey had taken her from rejecting religion in college, to a career in journalism that ultimately focused on the hope of faith as a devoted Catholic. Her activism landed her in jail twice. She had an abortion and ended a bad marriage, and later was in a common-law marriage for many years. Whether living in Hollywood or Mexico, she had a commitment to the poor, whatever the cost.

Dorothy Day's journey teaches us to see Christ in other people. That was her form of mysticism—not an easy form. She found that love of others can be a harsh and dreadful thing, but that is where we are going to find Christ.

FURTHER READING

Coles, Robert. *Dorothy Day: A Radical Devotion*. Reading, MA: Addison-Wesley, 1987.

Day, Dorothy. *The Long Loneliness*. San Francisco: Harper & Brothers, 1952.

12
DAG HAMMARSKJÖLD
1905–1961
A Hidden Mysticism

The engines of the U.S. military plane droned on as it continued its course to China. The diplomat on board had time on this long flight to ponder the situation—he was on his way to attempt a negotiation to release American airmen who were shot down during the Korean War. A Chinese court had convicted all eleven of them of spying, claiming they had violated Chinese air space. The United States insisted they were over North Korea. China had already been holding four other American jet pilots who had also been shot down, and the latest round of captives only served to further inflame the hostilities.

What would this diplomat say? What would his strategy be? How would he be received? His trip was controversial. The United Nations was about to pass a resolution condemning China for violating the Armistice Agreement by holding the airmen. China, for its part, wanted admission to the United Nations, but there was much opposition from many sources, and the diplomat knew he could not promise anything. He was a religious man,

Dag Hammarskjöld

and during the long flight he copied down in his journal verses from Psalm 139:

> If I take the wings of the morning
> and settle at the farthest limits of the sea,
> even there your hand shall lead me,
> and your right hand shall hold me fast. (vv. 9–10)

When the airplane landed in Peking, it was bitterly cold. The diplomat was Dag Hammarskjöld, the Secretary General of the United Nations, who soon met Premier Chou En-lai. Negotiations were long and delicate, and it would be many months before the airmen were finally released.

Hammarskjöld was an economist, a diplomat, and a religious mystic. After his mysterious death in a plane crash in 1961, while attempting to negotiate a peace in Africa, his journal was discovered in his New York apartment. It was later published under the title *Markings* and became one of the classic religious texts of the twentieth century. The book revealed to his closest associates that there was a religious side to the man they had never sensed. Religious feelings and experiences motivated his work, but few knew it.

Some were shocked by the journal. A review in *The New Republic* said that *Markings* was not what close friends had hoped for as a final testament: "Some considered it an embarrassment, not knowing what to make of so gratuitous an example of discrepancy, unreason, and excess, and the more they liked the man, the more they wish it had never happened."[1] In an article in *Look* magazine, critic John Lindberg described *Markings* as "the self-revelation of a man who in the end conceived of himself as a modern avatar, at the council table on the East River," and raised the question how it was possible "for this supposedly sober Swede to assume the role of savior on the rostrum of the

LONGING FOR GOD

United Nations without the spectators becoming aware of what was going on."[2]

Henry P. Van Dusen, president of Union Theological Seminary in New York, described Hammarskjöld as "one of the truly great men of this era," and "a Renaissance man of the mid-twentieth century."[3] Indeed, he had many interests: art, music, literature, mountain climbing, languages, economics, nature, and religion. He loved nothing more than intellectual conversation and regretted it when his friends married and were no longer available for discussions.

Hammarskjöld was born in 1905. His father was a rather unpopular prime minister of Sweden during World War I. He represented an old conservative Lutheranism and believed strongly that one should do one's duty. Dag Hammarskjöld's biographer, Sven Stolpe, described the elder as "a great but detested politician, with considerable resources and brilliant gifts, but with only meager capacity for making direct and warm contact with his fellow men."[4] His mother, on the other hand, had a more evangelical religious outlook and was attracted to the emotional rather than the intellectual side of religion. Dag went to church with her regularly, but his friends assumed it was out of courtesy to her. Someone that brilliant, they believed, would have no time for religion.

Hammarskjöld's father was the governor of Uppsala for almost twenty-five years. A major influence on Dag during those years was the archiepiscopal palace nearby. He was a childhood playmate of the children of Lutheran archbishop Nathan Soderblom, one of the pioneers of the ecumenical movement, who was responsible for a major conference on Life and Work held in Stockholm in 1925. The event was one of the milestones leading to the formation of the World Council of Churches after World War II. Hammarskjöld attended the conference as an usher. Henry Van Dusen told a story about someone suggesting that the general secretary of the World Council tell Hammarskjöld something about

Dag Hammarskjöld

the ecumenical movement. Hammarskjöld replied, "Oh, I know all about that. I was brought up under Soderblom."[5] Hammarskjöld attended the University of Uppsala, where he completed his bachelor of arts degree in two years. He studied literature, philosophy, French, and economics, but complained to Soderblom's wife, "I thought I should be reading about the progress of ideas through the ages, not wasting attention on the love affairs of authors."

During the 1920s, Hammarskjöld kept his religious feelings to himself. His companions would not be interested. Whenever he tried to talk about religious or metaphysical ideas, they had no idea what he was talking about and failed to understand him.

After completing a doctorate at the University of Stockholm, Hammarskjöld entered government service and rose rapidly through the ranks. He began working for the Royal Commission on Unemployment, soon became undersecretary in the Ministry of Finance, and later would hold the position of chairman of the Bank of Sweden.

He developed a reputation for hard work and excessively long hours. In 1946, he renegotiated a trade agreement with the United States and headed a delegation from Sweden that participated in discussions on the Marshall Plan. His next step was becoming vice chair of the Organization for European Economic Cooperation. In 1947, he joined the Ministry of Foreign Affairs in Sweden and was eventually appointed vice minister. Four years later, he became vice chair of Sweden's delegation to the United Nations, ascending to the chairmanship a year later. Finally, on April 10, 1951, after the resignation of Norway's Trygve Lie, he was elected to the first of two terms as Secretary General of the United Nations.

Soon after his election, he was a guest on Edward R. Murrow's radio program.[6] On the air, Hammarskjöld presented a statement, a credo, about his life and beliefs. He affirmed that he had inherited from his father's side of the family the belief in selfless service

LONGING FOR GOD

to country and humanity. From scholars and clergymen on his mother's side, he learned the gospel teaching that all people are created equal as children of God. While many of his Swedish friends assumed that he shared their agnosticism, his credo was a ringing affirmation of faith. He was attracted to the definition of faith used by St. John of the Cross: "Faith is the union of God with the soul." That is a classic mystical statement. Union with God is the ultimate desire of the mystic. Hammarskjöld was so devoted to that explanation that he returned to a variation of it in *Markings*: "Faith is the marriage of God and the soul."[7] Religious language, he said, is simply a "set of formulas which register a basic spiritual experience." It does not describe sensory reality. Hammarskjöld said that it took him a long time to reach that point in his thinking, but when he did, the Christian beliefs in which he had been raised became his by his own free choice.

Hammarskjöld told Murrow that there were two major religious influences on him that determined how he would live. The first was Albert Schweitzer, a multitalented missionary who ran a hospital in Lambarene, Gabon, a French colony in Africa. He was a physician, a talented organist, an authority on Bach, and a theologian and biblical scholar. Schweitzer taught him that "the ideal of service is supported by and supports the basic attitude to man set forth in the gospel." "In his work," Hammarskjöld said of Schweitzer, "I also found the key for modern man to the world of the Gospels."

Schweitzer's influence is an interesting part of Hammarskjöld's religious makeup. Van Dusen of Union Seminary reported that on a mountain climb in 1948, Hammarskjöld took along a bulky German volume in which he seemed to be deeply absorbed. It was the original edition of Schweitzer's *The Quest of the Historical Jesus*, and he suggested to his companions that they should read it.

There were many connections between Schweitzer and Sweden in the 1920s. When his hospital had financial problems,

Dag Hammarskjöld

Schweitzer received aid from Archbishop Soderblom. To raise additional money, Schweitzer played Bach organ concerts in Sweden, delivered the Glaus Petri Lectures in Uppsala, and became well known in Swedish circles. Hammarskjöld had ample opportunity to be influenced by Schweitzer.

There were two major ideas that Hammarskjöld received from Schweitzer. The first was a strong emphasis on ethics. In an article published in a Swedish journal called "The Civil Servant and Society," Hammarskjöld wrote, "The ethic exemplified by Schweitzer finds expression in the subordination of private interests to the whole: a moral obligation, first to the community in the sense of the nation; secondly, to the larger community represented by internationalism."[8] Van Dusen received a letter from Schweitzer saying that he had met Hammarskjöld in Switzerland and that they had similar views on ethics. Hammarskjöld was to visit Schweitzer's hospital at Lambarene on the Africa trip during which Hammarskjöld's plane crashed and he died.

A second influence from Schweitzer was an emphasis on the humanity of Jesus. When it was published in 1906, *The Quest of the Historical Jesus* struck the field of New Testament scholarship like a thunderbolt. Hammarskjöld was impressed with the effort to discover the historical Jesus, which presented a picture of him as "a human being, living and acting in a quite distinct historical situation." The reflections on Jesus in *Markings* are not written in lofty Christological language. Instead, they describe a man struggling with his mission and destiny. This was "the key for modern man to the world of the Gospels" that Hammarskjöld discovered in Schweitzer's writings.

Another important influence on Hammarskjöld that he mentioned on Murrow's program was the medieval mystics. Hammarskjöld makes references in *Markings* to Meister Eckhart, Thomas à Kempis, and St. John of the Cross. On the trip to Africa, he had with him a copy of *The Imitation of Christ*, a fifteenth-century spiritual classic designed to help a person

LONGING FOR GOD

deepen his or her spiritual life. Hammarskjöld said that the lesson learned from these mystics was "how man should live a life of active social service in full harmony with himself as a member of the community of the spirit."
The mystics taught him that self-surrender was the way to self-realization. It was singleness of mind and inwardness that "gave people the strength to say yes to every demand which the need of their neighbors made them face, and to say yes to every fate life had in store for them." "For them," Hammarskjöld said, "love is an overflowing of strength with which they felt themselves filled when living in true self-oblivion. This love found natural expressions in an unhesitant fulfillment of duty and in an unreserved acceptance of life, whatever it brought them personally of toil, suffering, or happiness." Hammarskjöld concluded his credo, "I know that their discoveries about the law of the inner life and of action have not lost their significance."

Another important influence on Hammarskjöld was the Bible. *Markings* contains quotes from twenty Old Testament psalms. Four of them, 4, 60, 62, and 73, are quoted twice. There are three quotations from the Gospel of John, and one each from Genesis, Isaiah, Matthew, and Revelation. There are several references to the Lord's Prayer.

While Hammarskjöld was steeped in traditional Christianity, his religious beliefs were anything but narrow. An important aspect of his faith was the universality of his religious outlook. He quoted from non-Christian mystics and spiritual writers. He said, "The lovers of God have no religion but God alone." He referred to Chinese, Greek, and Zoroastrian religions. He believed that no limits could be put on God's activity in the world. This universal activity could be recognized in non-Christian religions. Henry Van Dusen said that Hammarskjöld's faith was built on a sort of practical devotion and his own religious experience.[9]

This universal religious interest can be seen in one of his projects at the United Nations building in New York, the creation of a

Dag Hammarskjöld

meditation room. This was to be a place in the United Nations where people could find quiet for reflection and stillness. He supervised every detail of "A Room of Quiet," as it was called. The only symbol in the room was a shaft of light striking a piece of iron ore. This symbolized, he said, "how the light of the spirit gives light to matter." The stone may appear to be an empty altar, but Hammarskjöld said it is empty, "not because there is no God, not because it is an altar to an unknown god, but because it is dedicated to the God whom man worships under many names and in many forms." There were no other symbols in the room because he did not want anything to distract people's attention or disrupt the stillness within themselves. The simplicity of the room created an atmosphere of deep silence, where a diplomat or someone else could ponder not just the work he or she might be doing, but its significance for the whole world. The one symbol in the room had a universal significance, generating a hope for peace for all people.

Markings is a remarkable book, a diary of thoughts kept throughout Hammarskjöld's adult life beginning in 1925, although no entries are precisely dated before 1953. The entries are brief, a melding of prose and poetry. About three quarters through the book Hammarskjöld explained its purpose. These notes, he said, were "signposts you began to set up after you had reached a point where you needed them." They contained ideas that he believed strongly but did not want to speak about while he was alive. Now we have them, and they give us rich insights into the life of a remarkable man.

Hammarskjöld had a strong sense of vocation, and throughout *Markings* he described his goals. At the beginning of his journal, he wrote that he had a sense of being driven forward into the unknown. The way became more difficult. He had high expectations but wondered whether he would ever get where he was destined to go.

His goal was not just professional—instead, it embodied a mystical element, a search for a clear, pure note in silence. A major part of his vocation was his own self-development. "What you have to attempt," he wrote, is "to be yourself." And what kind of self did he want to be? He prayed that he might become "a mirror in which, according to the degree of purity of heart you have attained, the greatness of life will be reflected."[10] Success by itself, he believed, was not a worthwhile goal. He said to himself, "Never let success hide its emptiness from you, achievement its nothingness, toil its desolation. And so keep alive the incentive to push further, that pain in the soul which drives us beyond ourselves."[11]

Nevertheless, his hopes for life were joyful and rich. "To exist in the fleeting joy of becoming, to be a channel for life as it flashes by in its gaiety and courage, cool water glittering in the sunlight in a world of sloth, anxiety, and aggression. To exist for the future of others without being suffocated by the present." He praised the person who "has given himself completely to something he finds worth living for."[12]

Hammarskjöld had a strong sense of a Divine Presence. He believed that God was active in his life, even though things may not be going as he wished. "When in decisive moments God acts," he wrote, "it is with a stern purposefulness. When the hour strikes, He takes what is His. What have you to say? Your prayer has been answered, as you know. God had a use for you, even though what He asks doesn't happen to suit you at the moment."[13] Whatever success one has in life must be attributed to God. "Rejoice," he wrote, "if you feel that what you did was necessary, but remember, even so, that you were simply the instrument by which He added one tiny grain to the Universe He has created for His own purposes."[14]

During his years in diplomacy, Hammarskjöld was not an active churchman, and many people were surprised by the intensity of his religious feelings expressed in *Markings*. The book reveals, however, a strong and passionate desire to be open and receptive to God. In 1953, he wrote in his journal, "Not I, but God in me."[15] Ten pages later he wrote this 1954 entry:

Dag Hammarskjöld

Thou who art over us,
Thou who art one of us,
Thou who art—
Also within us,
May all see Thee—in me also,
May I prepare the way for Thee,
May I thank Thee for all that shall fall to my lot.
May I also not forget the needs of others,
Keep me in Thy love
As Thou wouldest that all should be kept in mine.
May everything in this my being be directed to Thy
    glory
And may I never despair.
For I am under Thy hand,
And in Thee is all power and goodness.[16]

On the same page he wrote, "The 'unheard-of'—to be in the hands of God. Once again a reminder that this is all that remains for you to live for—and once more the feeling of disappointment, which shows how slow you are to learn." Later he added, "So long as you abide in the Unheard-of, you are beyond and above—to hold fast to this must be the First Commandment in your spiritual discipline."[17]

Hammarskjöld offered a clear, mystical statement when he wrote that he believed an individual is strongest when he or she focuses attention on God, because God is within the person and the person is in God. One is strong and free because the self no longer exists. He was sure that the sense of morality in society would not exist had it not been for those who have forgotten themselves in God.[18]

He also expressed a strong desire for a mystical encounter. It involved breaking through a barrier that, when encountering reality, prevented him from encountering himself. He saw himself as being "at the frontier of the unheard of." A mystical

LONGING FOR GOD

encounter was like a deep-sea dive of which he was "afraid, by instinct, experience, education, for 'certain reasons,' of putting my head under water, ignorant even, of how it is done." Later, he attempted to clarify a mystical encounter. Understanding faith as "God's marriage to the soul," meant to Hammarskjöld that "God is holy in you." With this faith, he said, "in prayer you descend into yourself to meet the Other, in the steadfastness and light of this union, see that all things stand, like yourself, alone before God."[19] Then he admonished, "So live, then, that you may use what has been put into your hand." No one else knew it, but Hammarskjöld's work was grounded in his own mystical experience.

Near the end of *Markings*, in an entry dated Whitsunday (Pentecost) 1961, just a few months before his untimely death, Hammarskjöld wrote again about his spiritual conversion: "I don't know Who—or what—put the question, I don't know when it was put. I don't even remember answering. But at some moment I did answer 'Yes' to Someone—or Something."[20] What he realized was that his own life was meaningful and had a goal. He now knew not to look back nor worry about tomorrow. He saw that the Way, an early term for Christianity, "leads to a triumph which is a catastrophe, and to a catastrophe which is a triumph." The only elevation that is possible to a person is found in the depths of humility. Courage had no more meaning because nothing could be taken from him. As he continued on "the Way" he learned gradually that behind every saying in the Gospels "stands one man and one man's experience." That is also what stands behind the prayer that the cup might pass from him and the promise to drink it, and also each of the words from the Cross.[21]

The last years of Hammarsköld's life were particularly difficult. Communists made fierce attacks on him. During the summer of 1961, a civil war in the former Belgian Congo occupied

Dag Hammarskjöld

much of his attention. In September, he had flown to Africa in the hope of negotiating a peace agreement. He spent his last night with the UN mission to the Congo and left in that house a German copy of Martin Buber's *I and Thou* and his personal copy of *The Imitation of Christ*. He was using a typed copy of his oath of office as a bookmark.

The next day, the plane on which he was flying to Rhodesia to meet Moïse Tshombe, the president of Katanga Province, crashed under mysterious circumstances. The only survivor, a UN security guard, said that he heard explosions before the crash. Speculation has centered on possible sabotage or an attack by a fighter plane. Others thought it might have been pilot error on a landing approach. Whatever happened, the world lost a great statesman whose work was undergirded by a deep mystical spirituality.

Yet, he kept that mysticism a secret. How many other secret mystics are there out in the world? Surely more than we know. He was a brilliant student, intellectual friend, government official, and Secretary-General of the United Nations, and no one knew the depth of Dag Hammarskjöld's religious life.

In the context of a busy life with many responsibilities, a quiet mystical life can happen. Hammarskjöld had an acute sensitivity to people, to nature, and, obviously, to God. He found the right mentors: Albert Schweitzer and medieval mystics, including Meister Eckhart.

We all need a mentor or spiritual director on the faith journey. It may be a person we can meet with, or it may be a writer or writers who seem to understand where we are in our quest. Avoid people who have all the answers. Seek out those who understand that the inner life has a quality of mystery and who encourage us to keep seeking.

FURTHER READING

Hammarskjöld, Dag. *Markings*. Translated by Leif Sjöberg and W. H. Auden. New York: Alfred A. Knopf, 1964.

Van Dusen, Henry P. *The Statesman and His Faith*. Rev. ed. New York: Harper & Row, 1969.

13

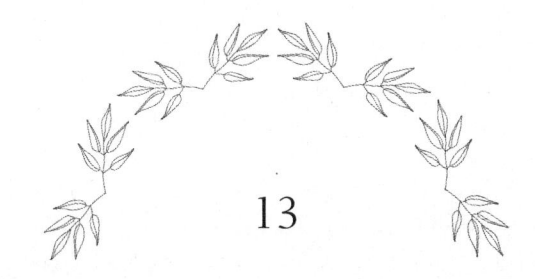

THOMAS MERTON

1915–1968
Always Searching

It was his turn to do the nightly fire watch in the monastery. He didn't mind it. In fact, he had written earlier, "The night, O My Lord, is a time of freedom."[1] After the monks had sung Compline, the last service of the day, and had gone to bed, he went to the familiar little box where the tools for this duty were kept. There was a pair of sneakers so he would not disturb the sleepers, a flashlight, a ring of keys, and a large clock with a leather strap that he wore over his shoulder. At various stations along the way, he would find a small key to punch the clock, leaving a record of his rounds.

From the deepest basements to the top of the bell tower, Thomas Merton could sense the history of the monastery. Founded in 1848 by a group of monks from France, the Abbey of Gethsemani is a remarkable place. The monastery in the rolling Knobs region of Kentucky near Bardstown was crowded with those who had been there for years and novices trying to find their way. He entered in 1941 and was now Master of Scholastics. As he

LONGING FOR GOD

walked down a hall, he remembered waxing the floor as a postulant, a new arrival not yet admitted as a novice. There were sounds in the night: empty choir stalls creaked, old boards sighed as the humidity changed, rusty hinges protested being bothered, and the sounds of nature outside came in through windows opened to catch a breeze. He thought of all the questions about God he had pondered, but had written in his journal, "I do not wait for an answer because I have begun to realize you never answer when I expect."[2] He later added, "There is greater comfort in the substance of silence than in the answer to a question. Eternity is in the present, Eternity is in the palm of the hand."[3]

As Merton made his rounds, he might have mused on his earlier life. His birth in Prades, France, in 1915 to artist parents, the birth of his brother, John Paul, the death of his American mother when he was only six, travels with his New Zealander father to Bermuda, France, and England so he could paint, and his father's death when he was sixteen. A kindly physician, a friend of his father, provided for his schooling in England, after which Merton found his way to Cambridge University, where he devoted most of his time to alcohol and sex. It was a terrible, disastrous year. When he visited his maternal grandparents in New York for the summer, the kindly physician wrote to him not to come back to England.

Now he had become a Trappist monk, living a life of prayer and silence, writing books and instructing the scholastics who want to be priests. How had he, the most unlikely candidate for the monastic life and priesthood, found his way to this place? Merton would go on to become one of the most influential spiritual writers of the twentieth century.

But back then, after settling in New York with his maternal grandparents, he enrolled in Columbia College (now University) where he became the proverbial big man on the campus. He joined a fraternity, wrote for the campus humor magazine, tried out for the track team, had a brief flirtation with Communism, edited the annual, and played jazz as loudly as he could. One of his friends said, "He was the noisiest bastard I ever met."[4]

He made important friendships at Columbia. Robert Lax, a poet, would be a lifelong friend and influence. Edward Rice would write the first biography of Merton, *The Man in the Sycamore Tree*.[5] Brahmachari, a Hindu monk, encouraged him to read the *Confessions* of St. Augustine and *The Imitation of Christ*. Merton's friend Robert Giroux later became an editor at Harcourt Brace, which would publish his early autobiography, *The Seven Storey Mountain*.

Merton liked Columbia. He said, "Compared to Cambridge, this big sooty factory was full of light and fresh air. There was a kind of genuine intellectual vitality in the air."[6]

Two professors influenced him in unexpected ways. One was Dan Walsh, whose course on theology was a turning point for Merton as he sought more knowledge about matters of faith. What impressed him about Walsh was that instead of teaching about various schools of thought and systems, he taught about Catholic theology in its wholeness. He saw various theologians as complementing each other, throwing diverse light on the same truths from different points of view.

The question is occasionally asked why Merton became a Catholic rather than a Protestant, which might have been a good fit for his free spirit. However, he was strongly attracted to the fact that Catholic theology was grounded in philosophy. He was impressed with Étienne Gilson's book *The Spirit of Medieval Philosophy*,[7] which emphasized the idea of God as pure Being. Merton said it was a relief to him to discover that no idea or image could adequately define or describe God. He later wrote that he acquired "an immense respect for Catholic philosophy and the Catholic faith."[8]

His other major influence was Mark Van Doren, a professor of literature. Merton was impressed by Van Doren's course on eighteenth-century literature—also the way he taught it, and his obvious love for the subject. One semester Merton signed up for a history course, only to discover that he had gone to the wrong room. Van Doren was about to begin his course on Shakespeare, so he decided to stay and see what it was all about. Merton said that it was the best course he had in college because he learned about what is really fundamental: "life, death, time, love, sorrow, fear, wisdom, suffering, eternity."[9]

Although no one was pushing him toward it, Merton began to think about conversion. He could see, on reflection, that God had been moving him toward a change in life for a long time, but he had not been able to sense it. After several hesitations, he walked to Corpus Christi Catholic Church next to the Columbia campus and took instruction. He saw his baptism as the beginning, not the end, of a spiritual life. At that point, he did not realize what a difficult journey it would be.

Merton was not drawn to the intellectual, dialectical, speculative theology of Thomas Aquinas, which he had learned from Walsh, but rather toward the spiritual, mystical way of Augustine. He received his bachelor of arts at Columbia in 1938 and began work on a master's degree, writing a thesis on William Blake, which he completed in 1939. He started on a PhD with a dissertation on Gerard Manley Hopkins, but never finished it. He was attracted to the mystical inclinations of these poets.

In the spring of 1939, Merton and his friend Robert Lax were walking down Sixth Avenue in New York. Lax asked Merton, "What do you want to be anyway?" Merton replied, "I guess what I want is to be a good Catholic." Lax replied, "You should want to be a saint." With the life he had been leading, Merton thought the idea was foolish. Lax told him that God would make him a saint if Merton would only let God do it.[10]

That summer, Merton, Rice, and Lax lived in a friend's cottage in Olean, New York, where they tried to write novels. Merton sent his to various publishers, but they all rejected it.

His days back in New York City were now filled with writing, friends, movies, beer, jazz, and dancing. A woman Merton was dating wondered if he would be happier as a jazz pianist than as a writer. One morning, following a long evening in a nightclub, after which friends slept over in his apartment, he awoke with a bad hangover and felt disgusted with himself. He was now beginning to think about becoming a priest.[11] When he mentioned it to Dan Walsh, Walsh said, "The first time I met you I thought you had a vocation to the priesthood."[12] He suggested that Merton look into the Trappists, but Merton said he could never live that life.

He did make an application to the Franciscans in New York, but when they learned of his Cambridge past, they decided he did not have a vocation. Meanwhile, he taught extension courses for Columbia, wrote book reviews, and had the good fortune to meet an agent, Naomi Burton, who would help him get published. She became a lifelong friend.

In the spring of 1940, he took a trip to Cuba. While visiting the town of Camaguey, he had a mystical experience of great importance. The setting was a Franciscan church. High above the altar where Mass was being offered was St. Francis with his arms raised to reveal the stigmata, the wounds of Christ in his hands and feet. As he entered, a group of school children filed in two-by-two, filling the first five or six rows. A Franciscan brother in a brown robe led the children in singing a hymn. Their voices were loud and clear and filled the church. The brother then led a recitation of the creed in Spanish, "Yo Creo…," ("I believe"), which the children began to recite.

At that point Merton said, "Something went off in me like a thunderclap," and without actually seeing anything, he knew with "the most absolute and unquestionable certainty" that God was right there before him, between him and the altar. The knowledge that heaven was there at that moment went through him like a flash of lightning that seemed to lift him "clean up off the earth," he wrote in his journal. It was not a sensory experience, but

LONGING FOR GOD

somehow he apprehended "God in all his essence, all His power, God in the flesh and God in Himself, and God surrounded by the radiant faces of...saints contemplating His glory and praising his Holy Name."[13] He knew that the experience was not the result of anything he had done or any particular virtue; it was only due to the kindness of God. It was a very intense experience, and it revealed his own sins more clearly than he had ever seen them before when compared with this act of mercy on God's part. He must have left the church buoyed by an overwhelming sense of mystery. Returning to New York, he and his friends went back to the cottage in Olean. Their previous summer there had been carefree, but this time World War II loomed, and the mood was more somber.

That fall, Merton became an instructor in English at St. Bonaventure College. His pay was forty-five dollars a month plus room and board. He enjoyed the Franciscan spirit of the college but did not see it as a permanent vocation. As the war in Europe expanded, he was required to take a draft physical but was rejected because of bad teeth. At the suggestion of Dan Walsh, he made a Holy Week retreat at the Abbey of Gethsemani, a Trappist monastery in Kentucky, arriving on Palm Sunday, April 5, 1941.

It was a powerful experience for Merton. The silence was overwhelming. Observing the monks chanting the psalms in the Divine Offices, as their services were called, touched him deeply. The simple food, the bare guest house room, the rigid schedule of the monks, created an atmosphere very different from the life he had been living. He began to see that the discipline of the life would give him a stability he had never had before. As the retreat ended, he said that the only thing he desired was to love God, and the only thing he wanted to do was to follow God's will. He wondered if this meant he should become a Trappist monk.

Meanwhile, he had become impressed with a Russian baroness, Catherine De Hueck Doherty, whom he had met when she spoke at St. Bonaventure. She founded Friendship House in Harlem to serve the needs of the poor. Merton visited, but decided he needed a situation where he would have time to write. He gave away most of his possessions, and on December 10, 1941, arrived by train at Gethsemani. It is not clear how Merton came to this decision. Some think that he was looking for stability in his disordered life. Although he took his new Catholic faith seriously, there was still some of the Cambridge behavior in his life. The rigors of the monastic life might teach him how to control his passions. So, Thomas Merton entered a monastery. His brother, John Paul, entered the Canadian Air Force.

Merton was interviewed by the abbot, Dom Frederick Dunne, and was accepted as a choir monk postulant. At this time there was a clear distinction between choir monks and lay brothers. The choir monks, whose most important function was liturgical, were priests or in the process of ordination, as Merton would soon be. He put on the white habit of a novice on February 21, 1942, and was given a new name, Brother, and, after ordination, Father Louis.

Gethsemani in the 1940s was a severe place. The abbot warned the novices that they had to look forward to sorrows, humiliations, fasts, and everything that human nature hates: the cross. In those days, monks slept on straw mattresses. The dormitory was a series of small cells separated by shoulder-high partitions. The place was cold in the winter and hot in the summer. The monks still slapped themselves with a small whip called the discipline on Friday while reciting the Lord's Prayer. In the Chapter of Faults, the monks "proclaimed" each other for breaking the rules, and each monk had to accept the penance given without question. Communication among the monks was by sign language. Mail was sent and received only four times a year. There was hard manual labor.

On the anniversary of his first visit to Gethsemani, Merton wrote that the monastery was the one place in the world "where everything made sense. Everything I wanted to do the most I can now try to do all the time without any interference. As soon as I got inside, I knew I was home."[14] That same year, 1942, his brother, John Paul, visited Merton at Gethsemani and was baptized a Catholic. The next year he was killed when his Canadian Air Force plane went down returning from a mission over Germany. In response, Merton wrote what many regard as one of his best poems, "For My Brother, Reported Missing in Action."

On March 19, 1944, Merton completed the novitiate and took simple vows, agreeing to stay for three more years. His first book, *Thirty Poems*, was published by New Directions. At the same time, urged on by his abbot, he began working on his autobiography, *The Seven Storey Mountain*. The book covers his life up to his entrance into the monastery. The title references Dante's *Purgatorio* and the seven levels of purgatory Merton believed he had to climb as he made the transition from his former life to the life of a monk.

The Seven Storey Mountain was published on October 4, 1948. Censors in the Cistercian order had reduced its length, and his friend Robert Giroux, at Harcourt Brace, made other suggestions. Initial sales were modest, but word began to spread. Eight months after its publication, Giroux presented Merton with the 100,000th copy. It was a bestseller and is still in print today.

The Seven Storey Mountain is the starting point for many who want to study Merton's thought. One of his more popular books is *New Seeds of Contemplation*, an expansion and revision of an earlier book, *Seeds of Contemplation*.[15] Here we find some of his basic ideas about mysticism which, in this book, he calls contemplation.

The first two chapters seek to answer the question, what is contemplation? Merton defined it as "the highest expression of (a person's) intellectual and spiritual life. It is that life itself, fully awake, fully active, fully aware that it is alive." Our life and being come from "an invisible, transcendent and infinitely abundant Source. Contemplation is, above all, an awareness of the reality of that Source."[16] That is what mysticism is all about, an encounter with God, the Source. It is beyond "reason and simple faith. It is a more profound depth of faith, a knowledge too deep to be grasped in images, in words or even in clear concepts."

Contemplation knows God "by seeming to touch him. Or rather it knows him as if it had been invisibly touched by him."[17] It is a gift of sudden awareness, "an awakening to the Real; within all that is real." It is a free gift of love, not something we can attain by intellectual effort. "It is awakening enlightenment and the amazing intuitive grasp by which love gains certitude of God's creative and dynamic intervention in our daily life."[18]

Chapter 2 tells us what contemplation (mysticism) is not. It does not provide us with a concept of God. What one experiences is inexpressible. It is not, Merton wrote, "a trance or ecstasy, nor the hearing of sudden unutterable words."[19] It is not the gift of prophecy or the power to read other's secrets. It is not an escape from anguish, conflict, pain, or doubt. It is the recognition that we know nothing about God because God is beyond all images, concepts, words, or rationalizations. The mystic finds that God is not a thing that can be defined. Rather, God is a "pure Who" who springs to awareness before our "inmost I."[20] For Merton, "no idea of Him, however pure and perfect, is adequate to express Him as He really is."[21] In contemplation we are simply lost in the mystery of God.

In an essay on "Contemplatives and the Crisis of Faith" in *The Monastic Journey*, Merton wrote that "all Christians are called to taste God." However, he added that "mystical knowledge...is not only an obscure knowledge of the invisible God. It is also an experience of God—a personal, loving encounter with one who has revealed himself to us."[22]

In a talk given to Asian monks in Bangkok, he said that inner transformation is what the monastic life is all about. "If you once penetrate by detachment and purity of heart the inner secret of the ground of one's ordinary experience, you attain to a liberty which no one can touch."[23] What Merton has to say here is really no different from what other mystics in this book have said over the centuries. The mystical experience opens us to mystery, the mystery of God who cannot be defined, described, or analyzed. That is why mystics cannot tell us much about their experiences. Many would say what they experience is the awareness of love. Their experience is seen as a gracious gift of a loving God. The mystic awareness of God takes one to a new level of depth, a depth far beyond religious diversity, doctrinal formulations, creeds, and ecclesial institutions. Merton believed that there is truth in all religions. He saw the weaknesses of his own Church just as Protestants see them in their churches. He searched beyond the boundaries and probed the mysteries.

One of the most quoted statements from Merton is found in *Conjectures of a Guilty Bystander*. After many years in the monastery, he had an occasion to be in downtown Louisville. There he had an experience that put his monastic life in a new perspective. While standing at Fourth and Walnut in an area crowded with many shoppers, Merton said, "I was suddenly overwhelmed with the realization that I loved all those people, that they were mine and I was theirs, that we could not be alien to one another even though we were total strangers."

This gave him a new perspective on his monastic life. The notion of a separate "holy" existence was an illusion. The idea that by making vows monks suddenly become a different species, pseudo-angels, spiritual men, or people of the interior life was just not true. Merton did not question the validity of his monastic life and vocation. He now realized, however, that he was still just a man. He concluded, "I have the immense joy of being *man*, a member of the race in which God Himself became incarnate.... If only everybody could realize this....There is no way of telling people that they are all walking around shining like the sun."[24]

The Merton bibliography is enormous and continues to grow. It includes books, articles, letters, journals, and unpublished material by Merton, as well as books and articles by others

Thomas Merton

about Merton. There is an International Thomas Merton Society, which attempts to keep up with new publications and foster scholarship on Merton. A Merton Study Center at Bellarmine University houses a huge collection of Mertoniana, and smaller collections exist at other colleges and universities.

Merton had many interests. He corresponded with people all over the world, from well-known poets and writers, to theologians, to a death row inmate, to high school students writing papers, and to individuals who could not believe in God. He received so many letters that occasionally he would have a general letter duplicated and sent to many on his list.

He was a very ecumenical person. He was not interested in councils of churches or other organizations promoting Christian unity. He thought conversations on spiritual matters could generate more unity than anything else. Although he converted in an era of Catholic triumphalism, he developed an interest in the Protestant tradition. He read and corresponded with major Protestant theologians, engaged in dialogue with Protestant seminary students, and had personal visits from Protestant thinkers, professors, and leaders.[25] His interests extended beyond Christianity. He wrote about Hinduism, Islam, Buddhism, Judaism, Taoism, and even Cargo Cults. Merton was a constant searcher. He was always looking for new ideas, new truths, which were not limited to doctrines, traditions, or cultures. He developed plans to move to Nicaragua, Chile, and Mexico, to create unique communities, but these never came to fruition. His abbot did not want to lose him, and Merton was obedient. He wanted to establish a monastic center where intellectuals could gather for dialogue, but it didn't happen. Early in his monastic life he had sought more solitude by requesting permission to transfer to the Camaldoli or the Carthusians, hermit orders, but permission was denied.

Eventually he was allowed to move into a small building on the grounds of the monastery that became his hermitage. It had originally been built as a place for ecumenical conversations with

Protestants. At first, he was allowed to spend only a few hours now and then in the place. Abbot James Fox gradually increased the amount of time and, finally, Merton was allowed to spend his last three years as a full-time hermit.

Eastern religions were a major interest of Merton's, particularly the Zen Buddhist version. His book *Mystics and Zen Masters* has essays on many religious traditions. One of the few times he was allowed to leave the monastery was for a brief trip to New York to visit D. T. Suzuki, one of the greatest Zen teachers of his time. Suzuki wrote a book comparing Buddhist mysticism with the mysticism of Meister Eckhart, *Mysticism: Christian and Buddhist*.[26] Merton had wanted to have Suzuki write an introduction to his book on the desert fathers, but the Cistercian officials denied permission. Merton's *The Way of Chuang Tzu* is a book about Taoism. He said, "I have enjoyed writing this book more than any other I can remember."[27]

Zen and the Birds of Appetite contains an essay on "Transcendent Experience." Merton defined transcendent experience as "an experience of metaphysical or mystical self-transcending and at the same time an experience of the 'Transcendent' or the 'Absolute' or 'God' not so much as object but Subject."[28] That sentence is packed with meaning. The experience is to discover the reality of all that is by transcending the self, that is the false self, or the no-self as Merton calls the self with whom we live, and becoming one with the Self of God in what mystics called the unitive way.

This is beyond the ordinary level of religious experience. Mystics talk about losing the ego-self or the annihilation of the ego. An encounter with God may seem to make the ego irrelevant as one becomes lost in the awareness of God. Merton put this into a Christian perspective. The experience for him is grounded in Christ or the Holy Spirit within us, whereby the mystic identifies with Christ. As St. Paul explained, "It is no longer I who live, but it is Christ who lives in me" (Gal 2:20). For Merton, it was a matter of having the mind of Christ (1 Cor 2:16; Phil 2:5). The mystic, Merton wrote, "is never purely or simply, the mere empirical ego." It is the person who is "identified with Christ, one with Christ."

How do mystics live? There is no one answer to the question, but we do get some help from Merton. One of his correspondents was a Pakistani, Abdul Aziz, a retired government official. He wanted to know how Merton spent his days in his hermitage. Merton gave a rather specific reply. His hermitage, he said, was about a ten-minute walk from the monastery, hidden in the woods. He went to bed about 7:30 p.m. and rose at 2:30 a.m. He read one of the Divine Offices, which the monks chant together seven times a day. Then he took an hour or so for meditation followed by Bible reading and a simple breakfast, mostly bread and tea or coffee. He read until sunrise for approximately two hours depending on the season.

At sunrise he read another Office and then engaged in manual work, which usually included cleaning the hermitage and chopping wood. At 9:00 a.m., it was time for an Office, after which he wrote a few letters. Then he walked back to the monastery to say Mass since he was not yet permitted to say it in the hermitage. He took one cooked meal in the monastery and returned to the hermitage.

In the afternoon, he did more reading, said the appropriate Office, and spent from one to two hours in meditation. Around 4:00 p.m., he prayed a final Office and prepared a simple supper. There was more time for meditation, and then he went to bed.

His meditation gave attention to the presence of God, God's will, and God's love. This was all based on a faith that is essential to knowing the presence of God. He did not imagine anything, nor did he have any precise image of God in his mind. Rather, Merton wrote, "it is a matter of adoring Him as invisible and infinitely beyond our comprehension." He described his prayer as "a kind of praise rising up out of the center of Nothing and

LONGING FOR GOD

Silence." He said that his prayer is not thinking about anything, but "a direct seeking of the Face of the Invisible, which cannot be found unless we become lost in Him who is Invisible."[29]

Merton received constant invitations to speak or attend conferences, but his abbot at the time always refused permission. However, when an invitation came to attend a meeting of Asian monks in Thailand in December of 1968, he received permission to go from a new abbot. The trip would involve much more than just attending a conference. He would visit Calcutta, New Delhi, the Himalayas, Madras, Ceylon (now Sri Lanka), and Bangkok. But for his untimely death, he would have visited Indonesia, Hong Kong, Burma, Nepal, and Japan. He wanted to meet as many religious teachers as possible: scholars, lamas, rimpoches (Buddhist spiritual masters), Zen masters, monks, sages, gurus, and rōshis.[30] His *Asian Journal* is a rich resource for understanding Merton. Here we learn why he was so attracted to Eastern religions, what he was ultimately seeking, and how he really understood religion. It contains not only journal entries but also some relevant letters and essays.

The *Journal* began with his takeoff in a Pan American plane in San Francisco. Merton wrote that at last he was on his "true way after years of waiting and wondering and fooling around." He made clear his purpose. "May I not come back without having settled the great affair." It is not clear what the "great affair" was, but there are hints now and then as the journey continued.

One of the highlights of the trip included a series of visits with the Dalai Lama. The first was on November 4, 1968, in the afternoon.[31] A long trip up a mountain in a Jeep took him to the Dalai Lama's palace, where Merton's passport was checked by an Indian official. Merton described the Dalai Lama as "most impressive as a person. He is strong and alert, bigger than I expected." He was a "very solid, energetic, generous, and warm person." The entire conversation was about religion, philosophy, and meditation. Merton talked about personal concerns and his interest in

Tibetan mysticism. The Lama suggested Eastern philosophies he should study and books he should read, and urged that Merton develop a strong grounding in metaphysics. He promised another conversation in two days.

In between those conversations, Merton thought about his own life and future. He gained a new appreciation for his hermitage at Gethsemani. It did provide solitude for the kind of study and meditation the Lama suggested. He also thought about moving to a hermitage in Alaska, where there would be fewer distractions and interruptions. There follows a series of quotations in his journal by a variety of Buddhists. Some of the rimpoches he consulted were opposed to absolute solitude and suggested that Merton should live in solitude for much of a year and then come out for a time. He believed that his recent days in India had been "extremely fruitful in every way." Here is much, he wrote, that he did not quite understand, but perhaps he did not need to understand. Although he expressed his love for Gethsemani and told the monks he would always be a monk of the place, he realized that he had needed to get away for a long time. His frustrations with Gethsemani and the Cistercian Order created a need to get into a different context and sort out many of his issues.

On November 6, he had his second audience with the Dalai Lama. There was some discussion of philosophical issues, and Merton had a bit of trouble getting the Lama to understand what he meant. But then they returned to the question of meditation. The Lama demonstrated the sitting position for meditation that he believed was essential. Next, the conversation focused on "concentrating on the mind." Merton called it a "lively conversation" that both men enjoyed. He wrote in his journal that the Lama "insists on detachment, on an 'unworldly life,' yet saw it as a way to a complete understanding of, and participation in, the problems of life and the world." He invited Merton to come back for a conversation about Western monasticism.

LONGING FOR GOD

Merton reported that his third interview with the Dalai Lama was the best. The Lama wanted to know about vows. Did Western monastic vows have any connection with spiritual transmission? Did Western monks, after making vows, progress spiritually toward "eventual illumination?" What methods of ascetic self-denial helped purify their minds of passions? He was more interested in the "mystical life" than in external observances. Why did monks not eat meat? What about alcoholic beverages and movies? Merton concluded, "It was a very warm and cordial discussion and at the end I felt we had become very good friends and were somehow quite close to one another." Merton wrote in a letter to Gethsemani, "I hope I can bring back to my monastery something of the Asian wisdom with which I am fortunate to be in contact."

One of the most puzzling and mysterious parts of Merton's journey was to the ruins of Polonnaruwa in Ceylon. Polonnaruwa was an ancient city, considered holy by Hindus and Buddhists. Merton noted that here there were "few people, no beggars, a dirt road. Lost." Then he found a monastic complex. There were ruins of palaces and temples. He was accompanied by the vicar general of the local diocese, who was suspicious of paganism. Fortunately, he hung back so that Merton could approach statues of the Buddha barefooted and undisturbed on the sand and wet grass. Merton was deeply moved by three colossal statues: a seated Buddha, a reclining Buddha, and a large statue of one of the Buddha's disciples standing by the head of the reclining Buddha.[32] He was moved by the "silence of the extraordinary faces. The great smiles. Huge and yet subtle. Filled with every possibility, questioning nothing, knowing everything, rejecting nothing, peace."

Merton wrote in his journal that he was "knocked over" by the obvious clarity of the statues, the shape, line, and design of them. He said that he was suddenly, almost forcibly, jerked clear out of his usual way of seeing things. Inner clarity seemed to explode from the rocks. There was at that moment "no puzzle, no problem, and really no mystery." He experienced "a sense of beauty and spiritual validity running together in one aesthetic illumination." People who have been deeply moved by Thomas Merton wish they knew that he meant when he said, "I know and have seen what I was obscurely looking for. I don't know what else remains but I have now seen and have pierced through the surface and have got beyond the shadow and disguise."

Like all mystical experiences, this one was impossible to describe. He said that he could not write about it. A man at a Buddhist university told Merton, "Those who carved those statues were not ordinary men."

From this experience it was on to Singapore and a brief visit with a professor of philosophy and his wife, then to Bangkok, Thailand, to attend the conference that was the original purpose of the trip. A Dutch abbot came to his hotel and took him to the Red Cross conference center where the meeting would be held, about thirty kilometers outside of Bangkok.

The last entry in the *Asian Journal* notes that it was the Feast of the Immaculate Conception, during which he would say Mass at St. Louis Church and then go to the Red Cross center. On the same day, he sent a letter to his secretary at Gethsemani, Brother Patrick Hart, which said, "I think of you all on this Feast Day and with Christmas approaching I feel homesick for Gethsemani."[33] At the conference, he gave a talk on "Marxism and Monastic Perspectives."

On December 10, 1968, Gethsemani received a cable from the American Embassy in Bangkok reporting that Thomas Merton had died. No one knows exactly what happened, but it seems that he went back to his room to take a shower and rest. Coming out of the shower still wet, he touched an electric fan that apparently had a short circuit in it. Merton's body was found lying on the floor with the tall pedestal of the fan across his body. His

LONGING FOR GOD

flesh showed some burns. The official cause of death was accidental electrocution.

Thus ended the life of a major twentieth-century spiritual influence. We wonder what more he would have done had he lived a longer life. There was sadness in Gethsemani and in the hearts of his many readers. His books continue to be read, however, and there are active Merton groups all over the world; new publications about him continue to appear; and Merton still changes people's lives. He brought mysticism into the twentieth century and at the same time his writings on racism, peace, and nuclear war have not lost their importance. We read them and they are so relevant that they sound as if they had been written today.

Merton's knowledge of the Christian mystical tradition was deep and broad, and he was beginning to explore the depths of mysticism in Judaism, Hinduism, Buddhism, Taoism, and Islam. All of this has resonated with people looking for more depth than traditional Western churches have had to offer. Those of us who love mysticism's potential owe Merton a great debt.

In many ways Merton's life parallels Augustine's: a life of dissipation without direction; a sense that there must be something better; and a faint interest in religion that ebbed and flowed, but mostly ebbed. If you were to read his writings in chronological order, which would be almost impossible to do, you would see a continuing evolution from conservative Catholic convert and Trappist monk to a man with an interest in Buddhism, Taoism, Islam, and Judaism, with a few curious digressions to groups such as Cargo Cults. His mentors ranged from his theology and literature professors at Columbia University to the great Zen Buddhist teacher D. T. Suzuki and the Dalai Lama. Merton corresponded with poets and writers all over the world and was always seeking new knowledge and new experiences. He crossed boundaries and left them behind. Yet, he continued to affirm his Christian faith even on the day of his death.

Thomas Merton

Thomas Merton calls us to continue to seek, to probe, and always to deepen our inner life for as long as we live.

FURTHER READING

Merton, Thomas. *The Seven Storey Mountain.* New York: Harcourt, Brace & Co., 1948.
Mott, Michael. *The Seven Mountains of Thomas Merton.* Boston: Houghton Mifflin, 1984.
Shannon, William H. *Silent Lamp: The Thomas Merton Story.* New York: Crossroad, 1992.

14

MYSTICISM AND ORDINARY LIFE

> Without any doubt, the mystery of our religion is great.
> —1 Timothy 3:16

What do these mystics have to do with those of us who live in the world? Many of us have families, mortgages, jobs, children to educate, people that need our care, and a variety of other responsibilities. Entering monasteries, living as hermits, and adopting voluntary poverty are not real options for most us. How do we find that spark, that ground of the soul, that inner light, that Divine Presence in our souls?

The ultimate goal of a religious person is to know and experience the presence of God at a very deep level. The key for mystics was the words of Christ from the Sermon on the Mount: "Blessed are the pure in heart, for they will see God" (Matt 5:8). We can all strive for that purity. It is a challenge in this world when there are so many forces vying for our attention and loyalty. The mystics call on us to stop and look at our values. What is most important

Mysticism and Ordinary Life

to us? Where does purity of heart rank? Taking a new look at this is important in any day, but the twenty-first century has presented us with a myriad of issues, problems, and challenges. The mystics saw virtue, living a moral and ethical life, as essential to the search.

The mystics have also taught us to deepen our understanding of God. The old man with a white beard seated on a golden throne might have served us well as an image of God when we were children, but the mystics have taught us that there is no language adequate to describe God and no image to help us see who God is. God is an indescribable mystery, more than we can ever imagine. God is beyond the limits of our sensory perceptions and beyond our powers of reason. Mystics often say that when they had an encounter with God, they did not see or hear anything but nevertheless were convinced beyond any doubt of God's presence.

The mystics we have studied in this book believed that contact with the Divine is made possible by an element of divinity deep within all of us. They called it the ground, the spark, the seed, the watermark, that part within us that is untouched by sin. The Quakers said that there is something of God in each of us. Dag Hammarskjöld wrote, "Thou who art also within us." Dorothy Day saw a Divine Presence in those who were poor, demented, and addicted.

There are two questions that are often asked about mysticism. The first is, can anyone describe a mystical experience? The consensus answer seems to be no. We do not have the language to describe it. When Paul said he had ascended to the third heaven, he said he heard things that cannot be told. There is no vocabulary for it. St. Bernard said he could not tell when it began and when it ended. Only those who have had the experience know what it was like and what it meant. It is impossible to tell another about it.

The second question is, can a mystical experience be created or acquired or is it a gift from God? Quaker mystic Douglas Steere wrote, "The weight is on the side of being utterly given."[1]

LONGING FOR GOD

An important element in our quest for God is an inner life of prayer, meditation, study, and silence. Regular prayer is very important, even though some days it will seem useless and dry. Often it will be rich. It is not any one experience of prayer or meditation that is important, it is the cumulative effect of these practices on our lives over the years that makes the difference. Structuring spiritual practices in our daily living stimulates growth and new insights. They do not have to be big productions; simplicity is the key. Start with something simple and build on it. Maybe a Psalm and the Lord's Prayer. Later, add a few minutes of silence. Then add a reading from one of the four Gospels. In time you may want to experiment with meditation. Use a worship service in church as a time for focusing more intently on God. Find your own way. Experiment and put aside what it not useful.

The point of such practices is to help us be more open and receptive to God. We may have attributed many incidents to chance, coincidence, or fate, when, later in life it becomes clear that God was acting in such events and we did not realize it at the time.

Developing a deeper inner life is not easy. Plotinus and others remind us that the falling and rising cycle is part of the process. At times God's presence in our lives is very real. At other times we seem to know God only by God's absence. Rich and dry seem to alternate in the spiritual life. We must be prepared for that and not give up.

A dominant characteristic of mystics was a deep longing for God. They wanted to know for sure that God actually exists, and they believed that it was possible for humans to have contact with the Divine. They were not seeking ecstatic experiences; they were seeking God. At the deepest level, they hoped for oneness, or union, with God. Experiences can be created, but we cannot conjure up God. Bernard of Clairvaux taught us how to love God. The best prayer we can pray is to express our love to God. Being a loving person opens us to the God who is Love. Some people

Mysticism and Ordinary Life

are hard to love. Dorothy Day knew that love in practice can be a harsh and dreadful thing compared to love in dreams. A historian once suggested to me that the self-denial demanded of us today is loving the unlovable. A pure heart is a heart of love.

Mystics saw whatever kind of relationships they had with God as a gift of love. We cannot create it. Meister Eckhart, Simone Weil, and Thomas Merton, among many others, were very clear that it was the love and mercy of God that enabled them to sense that Divine Presence.

Thomas Kelly gave us good advice when he said, "Walk and talk and work and laugh with your friends. But behind the scenes, keep up the life of simple prayer and worship." We don't need to make a big deal out of it, but in solitary, quiet moments, we probe our depths. The inner life is a hidden life. Paul said, "Your life is hidden with Christ in God" (Col 3:3).

Mystics had many practices. They spent time in silence, prayed the psalms, fasted, and believed that worship with others in church is important. They wanted a simple lifestyle. Their religion was not a leisure time activity—it was their life.

We have a great cloud of witnesses, a few of whom have been introduced in this book. We can learn much from them. They lived at different times, but what they have to teach us is timeless. Don't expect spectacular mystical experiences. Look for God in the ordinary, simple aspects of life, for God is at work there. You may well be taken by surprise.

NOTES

CHAPTER 1

1. Thomas Merton, *The Hidden Ground of Love: The Letters of Thomas Merton on Religious Experience and Social Concern*, ed. William H. Shannon (New York: Farrar, Straus and Giroux, 1985), 583.

2. W. R. Inge, *Christian Mysticism* (New York: Meridian Books, 1956), 5.

3. Bernard McGinn, *The Foundations of Mysticism: Origins to the Fifth Century*, vol. 1 of *The Presence of God: A History of Western Christian Mysticism* (New York: Crossroad, 1991), 44.

4. Origen, *An Exhortation to Martyrdom, Prayer and Selected Works*, trans. Rowan A. Greer, The Classics of Western Spirituality (New York: Paulist Press, 1979).

5. Quoted in Henri de Lubac, *Medieval Exegesis, Volume 1: The Four Senses of Scripture*, trans. Mark Sebanc, Ressourcement: Retrieval & Renewal in Catholic Thought (Grand Rapids: Eerdmans, 1998), 143.

6. McGinn, *Foundations*, 119.

7. Origen, *The Song of Songs, Commentary and Homilies*, Ancient Christian Writers, vol. 26, ed. Johannes Quasten, STD, and Joseph C. Plumpe, trans. R. P. Lawson (Westminster, MD: Newman Press, 1957), 21.

8. Origen, *The Song of Songs*, 60.

9. Origen, *The Song of Songs*, 63.
10. Elizabeth G. Vining, *Friend for Life: Rufus M. Jones* (Philadelphia: Lippincott, 1958), 51.
11. F. C. Happold, *Mysticism: A Study and an Anthology* (New York: Penguin Books, 1970), 18.
12. McGinn, *Foundations*, xv.
13. William James, *The Varieties of Religious Experience: A Study in Human Nature* (New York: Routledge, 2002; first published in 1902 by Longmans, Green, and Co., New York), 295.
14. Albert Schweitzer, *The Mysticism of Paul the Apostle*, trans. William Montgomery (New York: Henry Holt & Company, 1931), 2.
15. Schweitzer, *Mysticism of Paul*, 378.
16. Harvey Cox and Stephanie Paulsell, *Lamentations and the Song of Songs* in the series *Belief: A Theological Commentary on the Bible* (Louisville: Westminster John Knox Press, 2012), 171.
17. James, *Varieties*, 295–96.

CHAPTER 2

1. St. Augustine, *Confessions*, trans. Henry Chadwick, Oxford World's Classics (New York: Oxford University Press, 1992), 171.
2. Dom Cuthbert Butler, *Western Mysticism* (New York: Harper and Row, 1966).
3. McGinn, *Foundations*, 29.
4. See Garry Wills, *Saint Augustine*, for a popular account of Augustine's life (New York: Penguin Putnam, 1999).
5. Peter Brown, *Augustine of Hippo* (Berkeley: University of California Press, 1967), 21.
6. St. Augustine, *Confessions*, 2:2.

Notes

7. St. Augustine, *Confessions*, 2:9.
8. St. Augustine, *Confessions*, 3:1.
9. St. Augustine, *Confessions*, 3:7.
10. St. Augustine, *Confessions*, 3:7.
11. St. Augustine, *Confessions*, 3:11.
12. St. Augustine, *Confessions*, 5:10.
13. Butler, *Western Mysticism*, 36.
14. St. Augustine, *Confessions*, 5:11.
15. St. Augustine, *Confessions*, 5:19.
16. St. Augustine, *Confessions*, 6:1.
17. St. Augustine, *Confessions*, 6:7.
18. St. Augustine, *Confessions*, 7:10.
19. St. Augustine, *Confessions*, 7:16.
20. St. Augustine, *Confessions*, 7:24.
21. St. Augustine, *Confessions*, 7:27.
22. St. Augustine, *Confessions*, 8:18.
23. St. Augustine, *Confessions*, 8:17.
24. St. Augustine, *Confessions*, 8:29.
25. St. Augustine, *Confessions*, 7:16.
26. St. Augustine, *Confessions*, 7:17.
27. St. Augustine, *Confessions*, 8:6.
28. St. Augustine, *Confessions*, 9:10.

CHAPTER 3

1. Bernard of Clairvaux, *Sermons on the Song of Songs*, trans. Killian Walsh, OCSO, and Irene M. Edmonds, vol. 3 (Kalamazoo, MI: Cistercian Publications, 1976), Sermon 31; 137.

2. Emero Stiegman, an analytical commentary on Bernard of Clairvaux's *On Loving God* (Kalamazoo, MI: Cistercian Publications, 1995), 3.

3. Stiegman commentary: *On Loving God*, 3.

4. Stiegman commentary: *On Loving God*, 28.
5. Stiegman commentary: *On Loving God*, 29.
6. Stiegman commentary: *On Loving God*, 29.
7. Stiegman commentary: *On Loving God*, 30.
8. Stiegman commentary: *On Loving God*, 31.
9. Jean LeClercq, "The Making of a Masterpiece," Introduction to *Sermons on the Song of Songs*, vol. 4, by Bernard of Clairvaux, trans. Irene M. Edmonds (Kalamazoo, MI: Cistercian Publications, 1980), ix.
10. Bernard of Clairvaux, *Sermons on the Song of Songs*, trans. Killian Walsh, OSCO, vol. 1 (Kalamazoo, MI: Cistercian Publications, 1971), Sermon 2, 9.
11. Sermon 2, vol. 1:10.
12. Sermon 2, vol. 1:10.
13. Sermon 3, vol. 1:16.
14. Sermon 3, vol. 1:19.
15. Sermon 6, vol. 1:36.
16. Sermon 7, vol. 1:43.
17. Sermon 8, vol. 1:49.
18. Sermon 8, vol. 1:50.
19. Sermon 9, vol. 1:54.
20. Sermon 16, vol. 1:102.
21. Sermon 30, vol. 2:117–18.
22. Sermon 31, vol. 2:125.
23. Sermon 31, vol. 2:127.
24. Sermon 31, vol. 2:129.
25. Sermon 74, vol. 4:89–92.
26. Sermon 84, vol. 4:188.
27. Sermon 84, vol. 4:191.
28. Sermon 85, vol. 4:208.
29. Sermon 85, vol. 4:208.
30. Sermon 85, vol. 4:209.
31. Sermon 86, vol. 4:214–15.
32. Sermon 86, vol. 4:214.

33. Letter 146, *The Letters of St. Bernard of Clairvaux*, trans. Bruno Scott James (Kalamazoo, MI: Cistercian Publications, 1998), 214.

34. Letter 67, *Letters of St. Bernard*, 91.

CHAPTER 4

1. Barbara Newman, Introduction to *Scivias*, by Hildegard of Bingen, trans. Mother Columba Hart and Jane Bishop, in Classics of Western Spirituality (New York: Paulist Press, 1990), 18–19.
2. Bernard McGinn, *The Growth of Mysticism* (New York: Crossroad, 1994), 333–36.
3. Hildegard, *Scivias*, 59.
4. Hildegard, *Scivias*, 59–61.
5. Hildegard, *Scivias*, 73–85.
6. Hildegard, *Scivias*, 149.
7. Hildegard, *Scivias*, 150.
8. Hildegard, *Scivias*, 311.
9. Letter 390, *Letters of St. Bernard*, 460.

CHAPTER 5

1. Bernard McGinn, *The Mystical Thought of Meister Eckhart: The Man from Whom God Hid Nothing* (New York: Crossroad, 2001), 15.
2. Bernard McGinn, *The Harvest of Mysticism in Medieval Germany*, vol. 4 of *The Presence of God: A History of Western Christian Mysticism* (New York: Crossroad, 2005), 95.
3. Meister Eckhart, *Selected Writings*, trans. Oliver Davies, Penguin Classics (New York: Penguin Books, 1994), 3–52.
4. McGinn, *Mystical Thought*, 38.
5. McGinn, *Mystical Thought*, 31.

6. McGinn, *Mystical Thought*, 54–70.
7. McGinn, *Mystical Thought*, 35.
8. Meister Eckhart, *The Essential Sermons, Commentaries, Treatises, and Defense*, trans. Edmund Colledge, OSA, and Bernard McGinn, The Classics of Western Spirituality (New York: Paulist Press, new edition 1981), 243.
9. McGinn, *Mystical Thought*, 15.
10. Edmund Colledge in introduction to *The Essential Sermons, Commentaries, Treatises, and Defense*, by Meister Eckhart, 13–14.

CHAPTER 6

1. Henry Suso, *The Exemplar: Life and Writings of Blessed Henry Suso, OP*, trans. Sister M. Ann Edward, OP (Dubuque, Iowa: Priory Press, 1962), 1:7.
2. Bernard McGinn, *The Harvest of Mysticism in Medieval Germany* (New York: Crossroad, 2005), 195.
3. McGinn, *Harvest*, 197.
4. McGinn, *Harvest*, 206–7.
5. Susa, *The Exemplar*, 1:11.
6. Susa, *The Exemplar*, 1:11.
7. Susa, *The Exemplar*, 1:13–14.
8. Susa, *The Exemplar*, 1:37–38.
9. Susa, *The Exemplar*, 1:39–40.
10. Rufus Jones, *The Flowering of Mysticism: The Friends of God in the Fourteenth Century* (New York: Macmillan, 1939), 150.
11. McGinn, *Harvest*, 202–3.
12. Susa, *The Exemplar*, 1:15–18.
13. Susa, *The Exemplar*, 1:19.
14. Susa, *The Exemplar*, 1:144–46.
15. Susa, *The Exemplar*, 1:147–48.

Notes

16. Susa, *The Exemplar*, 1:152–53.
17. Susa, *The Exemplar*, 1:160–61.
18. Susa, *The Exemplar*, 1:167.
19. Susa, *The Exemplar*, 1:171.
20. Susa, *The Exemplar*, 1:174.
21. Susa, *The Exemplar*, 1:175.
22. Susa, *The Exemplar*, 2:39–40.
23. Susa, *The Exemplar*, 2:92.

CHAPTER 7

1. Thomas Merton, *The Sign of Jonas* (New York: Harcourt Brace, 1953), 20.
2. John Ruusbroec, *The Spiritual Espousals and Other Works*, trans. James A. Wiseman, OSB, The Classics of Western Spirituality (New York: Paulist Press, 1985).
3. Ruusbroec, *Spiritual Espousals*, 77.
4. Ruusbroec, *Spiritual Espousals*, 112.
5. Ruusbroec, *Spiritual Espousals*, 151.
6. Ruusbroec, *Spiritual Espousals*, 152.
7. Ruusbroec, *Spiritual Espousals*, 158.
8. Ruusbroec, *Spiritual Espousals*, 158.
9. Ruusbroec, *Spiritual Espousals*, 159.
10. Ruusbroec, *Spiritual Espousals*, 158.
11. Ruusbroec, *Spiritual Espousals*, 163.
12. Ruusbroec, *Spiritual Espousals*, 170.
13. Ruusbroec, *Spiritual Espousals*, 171.
14. Ruusbroec, *Spiritual Espousals*, 173.
15. Ruusbroec, *Spiritual Espousals*, 175.
16. Ruusbroec, *Spiritual Espousals*, 176.
17. Ruusbroec, *Spiritual Espousals*, 177.
18. Dom Cuthbert Butler, *Western Mysticism: The Teaching of Augustine, Gregory, and Bernard on Contemplation and the*

Contemplative Life (New York: Harper & Row, 1966, first published in 1922 by Constable in London), 210.

CHAPTER 8

1. Quoted in *Quaker Spirituality: Selected Writings*, ed. Douglas V. Steere, The Classics of Western Spirituality (New York: Paulist Press, 1984), 15.
2. Rufus Jones, *The Trail of Life in College* (New York: Macmillan, 1929), 159–60.
3. Elizabeth Gray Vining, *Friend for Life: The Biography of Rufus M. Jones* (Philadelphia: Lippincott, 1958), 135.
4. Rufus Jones, *Studies in Mystical Religion* (New York: Macmillan, 1947), 64.
5. Rufus Jones, *A Call to What Is Vital* (New York: Macmillan, 1947), 64–65. Visions were part of Hildegard of Bingen's mysticism, but Bernard of Clairvaux believed they were unnecessary.
6. Jones, *Studies*, 4–5.
7. Jones, *Studies*, 9–14.
8. Rufus Jones, *Some Problems of Life* (Nashville: Cokesbury Books, 1938), 136.
9. Jones, *A Call to What Is Vital*, 136.
10. Jones, *A Call to What Is Vital*, 140.
11. Richard M. Kelly, *Thomas Kelly: A Biography* (New York: Harper & Row, 1966), 34.
12. Richard M. Kelly, *Biography*, 37.
13. Richard M. Kelly, *Biography*, 51.
14. Richard M. Kelly, *Biography*, 91.
15. Richard M. Kelly, *Biography*, 91.
16. Richard M. Kelly, *Biography*, 92.
17. Richard M. Kelly, *Biography*, 97.

Notes

18. Thomas R. Kelly, *A Testament of Devotion* (New York: Harper & Brothers), 1941.
19. Thomas R. Kelly, *Testament*, 29.
20. Thomas R. Kelly, *Testament*, 39.
21. Thomas R. Kelly, *Testament*, 44.
22. E. Glenn Hinson, *Love at the Heart of Things: A Biography of Douglas V. Steere* (Wallingford, PA: Pendle Hill Publications, 1998), xiii.
23. Quoted in the foreword by E. Glenn Hinson in Douglas Steere, *Dimensions of Prayer: Cultivating a Relationship with God* (Nashville: Upper Room Books, 1997), xi–xii.
24. Douglas V. Steere, *Gleanings: A Random Harvest* (Nashville: The Upper Room, 1986), 81.
25. E. Glenn Hinson, ed., *Spirituality in Ecumenical Perspective* (Louisville: Westminster/John Knox Press, 1993), 6.
26. Douglas Steere, *Prayer and Worship* (New York: Association Press, 1938), 50.
27. Douglas Steere, *On Beginning from Within* (New York: Harper & Brothers, 1943), xiv.
28. Douglas Steere, *Work and Contemplation* (New York: Harper & Brothers, 1957), 49.
29. Steere, *On Beginning*, 12.
30. Steere, *On Beginning*, 88, 91.
31. Douglas Steere, *Together in Solitude* (New York: Crossroad, 1982), 10.
32. Steere, *Together*, 13.
33. Steere, *Prayer and Worship*, 11.
34. Steere, *Together*, 129.
35. Steere, *Together*, 134.
36. Steere, *Together*, 139.
37. Steere, *Dimensions of Prayer*, rev. ed. (Nashville: The Upper Room, 1997), xvi.
38. Steere, *Dimensions* (rev. ed.), 91.

CHAPTER 9

1. Howard Thurman, *With Head and Heart: The Autobiography of Howard Thurman* (New York: Harcourt Brace Jovanovich, 1979), 24.
2. Martin E. Marty, foreword to *A Strange Freedom: The Best of Howard Thurman on Religious Experience and Public Life*, eds. Walter Earl Fluker and Catherine Tumber (Boston: Beacon Press, 1999), xii.
3. Luther E. Smith Jr., introduction to *Howard Thurman: Essential Writings*, Modern Spiritual Masters (Maryknoll, NY: Orbis, 2006), 35.
4. Thurman, *With Head and Heart*, 44.
5. Thurman, *With Head and Heart*, 55–56.
6. Thurman, *With Head and Heart*, 76.
7. Thurman, *With Head and Heart*, 77.
8. Thurman, *With Head and Heart*, 95.
9. Thurman, *With Head and Heart*, 103.
10. Howard Thurman, *Jesus and the Disinherited* (New York: Abingdon-Cokesbury Press, 1949), 14–15.
11. Thurman, *With Head and Heart*, 129.
12. Thurman, *With Head and Heart*, 135.
13. Thurman, *With Head and Heart*, 168.
14. Thurman, *With Head and Heart*, 172.
15. Thurman, *With Head and Heart*, 226.
16. Howard Thurman, *The Creative Encounter* (Richmond, IN: Friends United Press, 1972), 37.
17. Thurman, *Encounter*, 20.
18. Smith, introduction to *Essential Writings*, 43.
19. Howard Thurman, *Disciplines of the Spirit* (Richmond, IN: Friends United Press, 1963), 9.

Notes

CHAPTER 10

1. Simone Weil, "Factory Journal," in *Formative Writings 1929–1941*, eds. and trans. Dorothy Tuck McFarland and Wilhelmina Van Ness (Amherst: University of Massachusetts Press, 1987).
2. William O. Paulsell, *Tough Minds, Tender Hearts: Six Prophets of Social Justice* (Mahwah, NJ: Paulist Press, 1990). Includes profiles of Martin Luther King Jr., Simone Weil, Dorothy Day, Dag Hammarskjöld, Dietrich Bonhoeffer, and Dom Hélder Câmara.
3. T. S. Eliot, Preface to Simone Weil, *The Need for Roots: Prelude to a Declaration of Duties toward Mankind*, trans. Arthur Wills (New York: Putnam, 1952), v–vi.
4. Mark Gibbard, *Twentieth-Century Men of Prayer* (London: SCM Press, 1974), 25.
5. Simone Pétrement, *Simone Weil: A Life* (New York: Pantheon Books, 1976), 114.
6. Gibbard, *Men of Prayer*, 26.
7. Weil, "Factory Journal," 225.
8. Simone Weil, *Waiting for God*, trans. Emma Craufurd (New York: HarperCollins Perennial Edition, 2009), 25.
9. Weil, *Waiting for God*, 26.
10. Weil, *Waiting for God*, 22.
11. Weil, *Waiting for God*, 26.
12. Weil, *Waiting for God*, 27.
13. Gustave Thibon, introduction to *Gravity and Grace* by Simone Weil, trans. Arthur Wills (New York: Putman, 1952), 5–6.
14. Weil, *Roots*, 43.
15. T. S. Eliot, preface to *Roots*, xii.
16. Weil, *Gravity and Grace*, 45.

17. Weil, *Gravity and Grace*, 47.
18. Weil, *Gravity and Grace*, 48.
19. Weil, *Gravity and Grace*, 53–54.
20. Weil, *Gravity and Grace*, 111.
21. Weil, *Gravity and Grace*, 163–64.
22. Weil, *Waiting for God*, 29.
23. Weil, *Waiting for God*, 57.
24. Weil, *Waiting for God*, 8.
25. Weil, *Waiting for God*, 13.
26. Thomas Merton, *Conjectures of a Guilty Bystander* (Garden City, NY: Doubleday, 1965), 30.
27. Francine Du Plessix Gray, *Simone Weil* (New York: Penguin Putnam, 2001), 207.
28. Gray, *Simone Weil*, 212.

CHAPTER 11

1. Robert Ellsberg, ed., *By Little and By Little: The Selected Writings of Dorothy Day* (New York: Knopf, 1983), 10–11.
2. Nancy L. Roberts, *Dorothy Day and the Catholic Worker* (Albany: State University of New York Press, 1984), 21.
3. Dorothy Day, *The Long Loneliness* (San Francisco: Harper & Brothers, 1952), 78.
4. Day, *Loneliness*, 139.
5. Dorothy Day, *House of Hospitality* (New York: Sheed and Ward, 1939), xiii.
6. Dorothy Day was editor and publisher until her death in November 1980. *The Catholic Worker* 29, no. 19 (July–August 1963): 3.
7. *Catholic Worker* 29, no. 10 (May 1963): 8.
8. *Catholic Worker* 37, no. 4 (May 1971): 2.
9. *Catholic Worker* 44, no. (May 1978): 8.

Notes

10. Fyodor Dostoyevsky, *The Brothers Karamazov*, trans. Constance Garnett, Modern Library (New York: Random House, 1950), 65.
11. *Catholic Worker*, 46, no. 9 (December 1980): 7.
12. Nancy Roberts, *Dorothy Day and the Catholic Worker* (Albany: State University of New York Press, 1984), 5.
13. *Catholic Worker* 27, no. 11 (June 1961): 2, 6.

CHAPTER 12

1. Dag Hammarskjöld, *Markings*, trans. Leif Sjöberg and W. H. Auden (New York: Alfred A. Knopf, 1964).
2. John Lindberg, "The Secret Life of Dag Hammarskjöld," *Look* 38, no. 13 (June 30, 1964): 37.
3. Henry P. Van Dusen, *The Statesman and His Faith*, rev. ed. (New York: Harper & Row, 1969).
4. Sven Stolpe, *Dag Hammarskjöld: A Spiritual Portrait* (New York: Scribner, 1966), 19.
5. Van Dusen, *Statesman*, 22.
6. Van Dusen, *Statesman*, 46–47.
7. Hammarskjöld, *Markings*, 97.
8. Van Dusen, *Statesman*, 106.
9. Van Dusen, *Statesman*, 192.
10. Hammarskjöld, *Markings*, 8.
11. Hammarskjöld, *Markings*, 55.
12. Hammarskjöld, *Markings*, 67.
13. Hammarskjöld, *Markings*, 89.
14. Hammarskjöld, *Markings*, 143.
15. Hammarskjöld, *Markings*, 90.
16. Hammarskjöld, *Markings*, 100.
17. Hammarskjöld, *Markings*, 101.
18. Hammarskjöld, *Markings*, 104–5.

19. Hammarskjöld, *Markings*, 165.
20. Hammarskjöld, *Markings*, 205.
21. Hammarskjöld, *Markings*, 205.

CHAPTER 13

1. Thomas Merton, *The Sign of Jonas* (New York: Harcourt, Brace & Co., 1953), 349.
2. Merton, *Sign of Jonas*, 358.
3. Merton, *Sign of Jonas*, 361.
4. Edward Rice, *The Man in the Sycamore Tree* (Garden City, NY: Doubleday, 1970), 25.
5. See James Harford, *Merton and Friends: A Joint Biography of Thomas Merton, Robert Lax, and Edward Rice* (New York: Continuum, 2006).
6. Rice, *Sycamore Tree*, 25.
7. Étienne Gilson, *The Spirit of Medieval Philosophy*, trans. A. H. C. Downes (New York: Charles Scribner's Sons, 1940).
8. Thomas Merton, *The Seven Storey Mountain* (New York: Harcourt, Brace & Co., 1948), 175.
9. Merton, *Seven Storey*, 180.
10. Merton, *Seven Storey*, 260.
11. Merton, *Seven Storey*, 276–77.
12. Merton, *Seven Storey*, 259.
13. Thomas Merton, *Run to the Mountain: The Journals of Thomas Merton*, vol. 1 (1939–1941), ed. Patrick Hart, OCSO (San Francisco: HarperSanFransico, 1995), 218. See also *The Secular Journal of Thomas Merton* (Garden City, NY: Doubleday, 1969), 76–78.
14. Jim Forest, *Living with Wisdom: A Life of Thomas Merton*, rev. ed. (Maryknoll, NY: Orbis, 2008), 81.

Notes

15. Thomas Merton, *New Seeds of Contemplation* (New York: New Directions Books, 1962).
16. Merton, *New Seeds*, 1.
17. Merton, *New Seeds*, 2–3.
18. Merton, *New Seeds*, 5.
19. Merton, *New Seeds*, 10.
20. Merton, *New Seeds*, 13.
21. Merton, *New Seeds*, 15.
22. Thomas Merton, "Contemplatives and the Crisis of Faith," in *The Monastic Journey*, ed. Brother Patrick Hart, OSCO (Kansas City: Sheed, Andrews and McMeel, 1977), 176–77.
23. Quoted in "The Monk" by John Eudes Bamberger in *Thomas Merton: A Monastic Tribute*, ed. Brother Patrick Hart, OSCO (New York: Sheed & Ward, 1974), 56.
24. Thomas Merton, *Conjectures of a Guilty Bystander* (Garden City, NY: Doubleday, 1966), 140–41.
25. See William Oliver Paulsell, *Merton and the Protestant Tradition*, The Fons Vitae Thomas Merton series (Louisville: Fons Vitae, 2017).
26. D. T. Suzuki, *Mysticism: Christian and Buddhist* (New York: Dell, 1961).
27. Thomas Merton, *The Way of Chuang Tzu* (New York: New Directions, 1969), 10.
28. Thomas Merton, *Zen and the Birds of Appetite* (New York: New Directions, 1968), 71.
29. Thomas Merton, *The Hidden Ground of Love: The Letters of Thomas Merton on Religious Experience and Social Concerns*, ed. William H. Shannon (New York: Farrar, Straus & Giroux, 1985), 62–64.
30. Brother Patrick Hart, in "Foreword" to *The Asian Journal of Thomas Merton* by Thomas Merton, ed. Brother Patrick Hart, James Laughlin, et al (New York: New Directions, 1968), xxiv–xxv.
31. Merton, *Asian Journal*, 100–125.

32. Merton, *Asian Journal*, 233–36.
33. Merton, *Asian Journal*, 257.

CHAPTER 14

1. Douglas Steere, *Together in Solitude* (New York: Crossroad, 1982), 139.